How to Sell to the U.S. Military

Learn How to Bid and Win Lucrative Government Contracts

by

Brian Cook

Table of Contents

Chapter 1:

GETTING READY TO DO BUSINESS WITH THE U.S. MILITARY

INTRODUCTION

The DoD is ready to do business, on a competitive basis, with competent firms that can supply the products or services it needs. Defense purchasing activities are particularly interested in establishing contacts with small business firms, small disadvantaged business firms, and women-owned small business firms.

Interested firms must help themselves by learning how DoD conducts its business, and by seeking out those military purchasing offices that buy the products and services they can supply.

Actually, there are few differences between your commercial business and selling your products or services to the various DoD organizations. Basic principles followed in selling within the commercial business field generally apply in dealing with DoD. Two principles especially appropriate in establishing and keeping a working relationship with military purchasing activities are:

- Learn both the needs and the buying practices of your potential customer.
- Follow leads on where buying is done, and seek sales opportunities throughout DoD.

This report is intended to provide firms that have little or no experience in selling to DoD with basic information about how DoD conducts its business, and with specific information for locating sales opportunities.

DoD CONTRACTING PRINCIPLES AND PRACTICES

The basic contracting rules for all Federal Government agencies are set forth in the Federal Acquisition Regulation (FAR). Additional rules unique to DoD are set forth in the DoD FAR Supplement (DFARS). These publications can be reviewed at any DoD purchasing or contract administration office, at any Small Business Administration (SBA) office, and at many local libraries (where they are known as Chapters 1 and 2 of Title 48 of the Code of Federal Regulations). The FAR and DFARS are also available on numerous world wide websites, including the OSD website (http://www.acq.osd.mil). To be a successful Defense contractor, you must have a working knowledge of both of these regulations.

How DoD Buys

Almost 98 percent of DoD's purchase transactions are for $100,000 or less. Although they account for less than 20 percent of DoD's procurement dollars, they total in the billions of dollars each year. Most of these millions of actions are accomplished using simplified acquisition procedures. Oral solicitations or very brief written requests for quotations are issued to prospective suppliers in the local purchasing area. The successful quoter is issued a purchase order, and compliance with the order (i.e., delivering the product or performing the service) constitutes contract acceptance and fulfillment.

Purchases over $100,000 are made by sealed bidding by competitive proposals, or (in unusual circumstances only) by other-than-competitive procedures. Sealed bids are used when the Government knows exactly what it needs, while competitive proposals allow flexibility in defining the exact requirement or the terms and conditions of the procurement.

Procurement by sealed bidding begins with the issuance of an invitation for bids (IFB) containing all the information bidders need to respond. The IFB states the needs of the purchasing activity and defines the work in sufficient detail to permit all bidders to compete on the same basis. It also identifies all factors to be considered in evaluating the bids. A standard form is provided on which bids are submitted, and a specific time is set for bid opening. The opening is held in public (you can attend), and the contract is awarded to that responsible bidder whose bid offers the best value to the Government.

When sealed bids are not appropriate, competitive proposals are solicited. The purchasing office issues a request for proposals (RFP). After reviewing the proposals received, the contracting officer ordinarily will negotiate with those suppliers that have submitted acceptable proposals, seeking the most advantageous best value contract for the Government.

Types of Contracts

DoD generally uses fixed-price contracts to acquire products and services. Cost-reimbursement contracts are used only when fixed-price contracts are not feasible. Most research and development (R&D) contracts are of the cost-reimbursement type. Fees under cost-reimbursement contracts are either fixed at the outset or subject to adjustment in accordance with a formula established in the contract. When unusual circumstances exist, a letter of intent may be used to authorize a contractor to start work before the final contract is executed.

Special Help for Small Businesses

It is national policy that a fair proportion of the products and services used by DoD shall be purchased from small, small disadvantaged, and women-owned small businesses. Certain factors limit DoD's ability to contract with small business. Vast amounts of facilities and working capital are required to produce major weapons systems. In many cases, even the resources of large business can be strained by performance and cost risks. To offset these factors, DoD has implemented a major program to ensure the award of a fair proportion of its contracts to small businesses. This program includes special personnel to assist small businesses, and the following purchasing procedures:

- Permitting offers on less than the total requirements and allowing the maximum time possible for preparation of offers.
- Setting aside, for award to small business only, any procurements where there is a reasonable expectation that at least two responsible small businesses will offer the products of small business concerns at reasonable prices. Most purchases under $100,000 are reserved for competition among small business only.
- Setting aside a portion of a procurement that would otherwise be too large for a total small business set-aside. Any business, large or small can compete for the non set-aside portion. Small business is then given the opportunity to receive a contract for the set-aside portion at the price of the non set-aside portion.
- Having the SBA review a small business' capability in the event the contracting officer determines it to be nonresponsible (see Preaward Determination of Responsibility below).
- Encouraging large DoD contractors to subcontract with small, small disadvantaged and women-owned small businesses.

In addition to helping all small business firms, DoD provides special emphasis to increase participation by small disadvantaged business firms. The main features are as follows:

- Seeking small disadvantaged business firms to supply the needed products and services, and setting aside for small disadvantaged business firms those solicitations where DoD can expect to obtain satisfactory performance, adequate competition, and a reasonable price from among the respondents.
- Contracting directly with the SBA, which will then subcontract the work to small businesses certified by the SBA as being socially and economically disadvantaged. DoD and SBA identify products and services that can be provided by small disadvantaged businesses that have an SBA-approved business development plan. The FAR (Subpart 19.8) provides detailed information on this procedure.
- Encouraging special attention to small disadvantaged business firm by DoD's large prime contractors in their programs of subcontracting.

Preaward Determination of Responsibility

DoD awards contracts only to contractors found to be responsible. The purchasing activity must evaluate the offerors in order to make a positive finding as to responsibility.

Getting accepted as a "responsible" contractor is not like getting on a qualified products list. You can't arrange for a survey at your convenience and wait until you are approved before submitting an offer. The determination of responsibility is done only in connection with an offer when you are the apparent low or otherwise successful offeror. To be found responsible, you must be able to demonstrate that you (1) have, or are able to obtain, adequate financial resources; (2) are able to comply with the delivery requirements; (3) have a satisfactory record of performance; (4) have a satisfactory record of integrity and business ethics; (5) have, or are able to obtain, the necessary organization, experience, accounting and operational controls, and technical skills; (6) have, or are able to obtain, the necessary production, construction, and technical equipment and facilities; and (7) are otherwise qualified and eligible to receive an award under applicable laws and regulations.

Sometimes a contracting officer proposes to reject the apparent successful offer of a small business firm because of doubt as to whether the firm is sufficiently responsible to perform the contract. In that event, the case must be referred to the SBA. If the SBA determines that the small business firm is responsible, it issues a Certificate of Competency (CoC) to the contracting officer, who then must award the contract to the small business firm.

THE DoD SYSTEM OF SPECIFICATIONS AND STANDARDS

DoD has exact specifications for many of the products and services it buys repeatedly. You should be familiar with the types of specifications, and you should know how to obtain them. Specifications are comprehensive descriptions of the technical requirements for material, equipment, and services. In addition to its specifications, DoD uses standards that establish the engineering and technical limitations and applications of items, materials, processes, methods, and engineering practices. Standards are used to ensure maximum uniformity in materials and equipment and to foster interchangeability of parts used in these products. Standards may be separately stated in a description of a need, but frequently they are also included in military specifications. Though use of Military specifications and standards continues within DoD, there is increasing emphasis on maximizing the utilization of commercial specifications and standards whenever practicable.

How to Acquire Specifications
Department of Defense Single Stock Point (DoDSSP) was created to centralize the control, distribution, and access to the extensive collection of Military Specifications, Standards, and related standardization documents either prepared by or adopted by the DoD. The DODSSP mission and responsibility was assumed by the Defense Automated Printing Service (DAPS) Philadelphia Office, in October 1990.

The responsibilities of the DODSSP include electronic document storage, indexing, cataloging, maintenance, publish-on-demand, distribution, and sale of Military Specifications, Standards, and related standardization documents and publications comprising the DODSSP Collection. The DODSSP also maintains the Acquisition Streamlining and Standardization Information System (ASSIST) management/research database.

Document Categories in the DODSSP Collection:
Military / Performance / Detail Specifications

Military Standards
DoD-adopted Non-Government / Industry Specifications and Standards
Federal Specifications and Standards
Military Handbooks
Qualified Products / Manufacturer's Lists (QPLs/QMLs)
USAF / USN Aeronautical Standards / Design Standards
USAF Specifications Bulletins

Although the DODSSP Collection contains over 50,000 line items, not all documents specified in Government procurements are included (e.g.: engineering drawings, some Departmental documents, and the majority of all Non-Government / Industry Standards). The Department of Defense Index of Specifications and Standards (DODISS) contains the complete list of Standardization documents in the DODSSP Collection.

This reference publication is available online to all ASSIST subscribers, on CD-ROM for single issue or subscription purchase or in paper format from the Superintendent of Documents:

Superintendent of Documents
U.S. Government Printing Office
Washington, DC 20402
(202)512-1800

A complete and descriptive list of products and services is available electronically on the World Wide Web at: http://www.dodssp.daps.mil or contact:

DoDSSP
Standardization Document Order Desk
700 Robbins Avenue, Bldg. 4D
Philadelphia, PA 19111-5094
(215)697-2667/2179

Acquisition Streamlining & Standardization Information System (ASSIST)
ASSIST is a database system for DOD-wide standardization information management. The ASSIST database system resides at the DODSSP, located at the Defense Automated Printing Service (DAPS) in Philadelphia, Pennsylvania.

ASSIST-Online is a Windows-based version accessible via Telenet. It is comprised of four parts: The Department of Defense Index of Specifications and Standards (DODISS), the SD-1 Standardization Directory, the SD-4 Status of Standardization Projects, and the Acquisition Management Source Data List (AMSDL). ASSIST Online is available as a yearly subscription service. The ASSIST-Online subscription includes a copy of the current ASSIST Computer base Training (CBT) CD.

The DODSSP also offers an ASSIST-CD. This standalone product consists of primary DODISS information and selected DODSSP document information, and boasts extensive report-generation capabilities.

Department of Defense Index of Specifications and Standards (DODISS)

The DODISS, as its name implies, is a comprehensive index of Federal and Military specifications and standards, guide specifications, military handbooks and bulletins, Commercial Item Descriptions, adopted non-government standards, and other related standardization documents used by the Department of Defense, and all available in the DODSSP Collection. It is an invaluable reference tool for anyone interested in identifying specific standardization documents for purchase.

The DODSSP issues complete revisions of the DODISS every other month, and several formats are available. The DODISS is available on CD-ROM, in standard Portable Document Format , with the appropriate reader software included; this product can be ordered either in single issue or as a yearly subscription with bi-monthly issues. The DODISS is also available on-line as a part of the ASSIST Standardization Document Management Database, and can be ordered with your ASSIST subscription. Finally, The Superintendent of Documents offers the DODISS in printed form.

Data Item Descriptions (DIDs)

Data Item Descriptions define the data required of a contractor in order to perform for a government contract. DIDs specifically define the data content, preparation instructions, format, and intended use.

The DODSSP issues DIDs as a complete set twice a year, in April and October. Included in this DIDs set is a current index of all active and cancelled DIDs - called the Acquisition Management System and Data Requirements Control List (otherwise known as the AMSDL 5010.12L). The complete DIDs set (with the AMSDL) can be ordered in paper format.

Annual subscriptions of DIDs updates are also available.

Mail Subscription Requests to:

DoDSSP
Standardization Document Order Desk
700 Robbins Avenue, Bldg. 4D
Philadelphia, PA 19111-5094
Phone : (215) 697-2667/2179

Contractors using the subscription service are not relieved of any responsibilities in complying with military contracts.

Special Assistance Desk - A special assistance desk is available Monday through Friday 7:30 AM to 4:30 PM (Eastern Time) to assist you in matters such as: Inquiries about

DoDSSP services, status of orders previously placed; establishing a customer account; sources for documents not at the DoDSSP; and special requests such as obtaining a complete set of documents.

Special Assistance Desk
(215) 697-2667/2179
7:30 AM to 4:30 PM (Eastern Time)
Note: Orders not accepted on these lines

or write to:
DoDSSP
Special Assistance Desk
700 Robbins Avenue, Bldg. 4D
Philadelphia, PA 19111-5094

Order Forms
Orders for individual documents can be made by using the DODSSP Specifications and Standards Order Form (DAPS-Philadelphia 1425/7).

Orders for all other DODSSP products can be made by using the DODSSP Products/ Subscriptions Order Form (DAPS-Phila 5270/5). These downloadable order forms in Portable Document Format (.pdf) can be accessed using Adobe's free Acrobat Reader Version 3.0 or later.

You will find that these forms are interactive, with various "live" buttons and text fields allowing you to complete them on-screen. Currently, your only options for submitting these forms are by mail or fax. Address and fax information is on the forms.

If you prefer, mail or FAX orders can also be made on official company letterhead.

The Federal Supply System
The Federal Government buys, stocks, and uses over 7 million items. As a prospective supplier, you should know some basics about the system that manages those items.

The catalog of the supply systems assigns National Stock Numbers (NSNs) to each item the Government uses. The NSN is a 13 digit number assigned by the Defense Logistics Service Center (DLSC), Battle Creek, Michigan. The first four digits identifies the Federal Supply Class (FSC (FSC) of the product. The next nine numbers represent the National Item Identification

Number (NIIN). The first two numbers of the NIIN identifies the country of origin. The remaining seven digits identifies the specific item. DLSC currently lists over 7 million NSNs. For information on NSNs, telephone customer service, (616) 961-4725; for NATO countries telephone (616) 961-4334.

The FSC system has three major subdivisions, which are dealt with in three different ways. The first major subdivision is R&D. See Part 3 of this special report for information about contracts for R&D.

All other services - as distinguished from R&D - are coded, in the FSC system, with a code that consists of one letter and three digits. The initial letter serves to group similar services. Table 1 lists these service group identifiers. These groups are subdivided, sometimes into only a few specific codes and sometimes into many. You should know which letter group seems to cover the service you can furnish.

TABLE 1: FEDERAL SUPPLY
CLASSIFICATION GROUPS
(for services other than research and development)

FSC Group	Description
B	Special Studies and Analyses - Not R&D
C	Architect and engineering Services - construction
D	Automatic Data Processing and Telecommunication Services
E	Purchase of Structures and Facilities
F	Natural Resources And Conservation Services
G	Social Services
H	Quality Control, Testing, And Inspection Services
J	Maintenance, Repair, And Rebuilding Of Equipment
K	Modification Of Equipment
L	Technical Representative Services
M	Operation Of Government-Owned Facilities
N	Installation Of Equipment
P	Salvage Services
Q	Medical Services
R	Professional, Administrative, And Management Support Services
S	Utilities And Housekeeping Services
T	Photographic, Mapping, Printing, And Publication Services
U	Education And Training Services
V	Transportation, Travel And Relocation Services
W	Lease Or Rental Of Equipment
X	Lease Or Rental Of Facilities

| Y | Construction Of Structures And Facilities |
| Z | Maintenance, Repair, Or Alteration Of Real Property |

The FSC system is most important to you in connection with DoD acquisitions of supplies and equipment. Here the identification is either by two-digit groups or by four-digit individual codes. Table 2 lists the two-digit groups. The listing of products and services in Part 2 of this special report is arranged in FSC sequence. Sometimes only the two-digit code is used; this means that, in general, the same major buying offices buy most of the products in the group. In other cases, some or all of the four-digit codes are listed; this means that there are differences in buying patterns. You should know at least the two-digit code, and preferably the four-digit code, covering each of your products.

TABLE 2: FEDERAL SUPPLY CLASSIFICATION GROUPS
(for supplies and equipment)

FSC Group	Description
10	Weapons
11	Nuclear ordnance
12	Fire control equipment
13	Ammunition and explosives
14	Guided missiles
15	Aircraft and airframe structural components
16	Aircraft components and accessories
17	Aircraft launching, landing, and ground handling equipment
18	Space vehicles
19	Ships, small craft, pontoons, and floating docks
20	Ship and marine equipment
22	Railway equipment
23	Ground effect vehicles, motor vehicles, trailers, and cycles
24	Tractors
25	Vehicular equipment components
26	Tires and tubes
27	
28	Engines, turbines, and components
29	Engine accessories

30	Mechanical power transmission equipment
31	Bearings
32	Woodworking machinery and equipment
34	Metalworking machinery
35	Service and trade equipment
36	Special industrial machinery
37	Agricultural machinery and equipment
38	Construction, mining, excavating, and highway maintenance equipment
39	Materials handling equipment
40	Rope, cable, chain, and fittings
41	Refrigeration, air conditioning, and air circulating equipment
42	Fire fighting, rescue, safety equipment and environmental protection equipment and materials
43	Pumps and compressors
44	Furnace, steam plant, and drying equipment; nuclear reactors
45	Plumbing, heating, and waste disposal equipment
46	Water purification and sewage treatment equipment
47	Pipe, tubing, hose, and fittings
48	Valves
49	Maintenance and repair shop equipment
51	Hand tools
52	Measuring tools
53	Hardware and abrasives
54	Prefabricated structures and scaffolding
55	Lumber, mill work, plywood, and veneer
56	Construction and building material
58	Communication, detection, and coherent radiation equipment
59	Electrical/electronic equipment components
60	Fiber optics materials, components, assemblies and accessories
61	Electric wire and power distribution equipment
62	Lighting fixtures and lamps
63	Alarm, signal, and security detection systems
65	Medical, dental, and veterinary equipment and supplies

66	Instruments and laboratory equipment
67	Photographic equipment
68	Chemicals and chemical products
69	Training aids and devices
70	General-purpose automatic data processing (ADP) equipment (including firmware), software, supplies, and support equipment
71	Furniture
72	Household and commercial furnishings and appliances
73	Food preparation and serving equipment
74	Office machines, text processing systems and visible record equipment
75	Office supplies and devices
76	Books, maps, and other publications
77	Musical instruments, phonographs, and home type radios
78	Recreation and athletic equipment
79	Cleaning equipment and supplies
80	Brushes, paints, sealers, and adhesives
81	Containers, packaging, and packing supplies
83	Textiles, leather, furs, apparel, and shoe findings, tents and flags
84	Clothing, individual equipment, and insignia
85	Toiletries
87	Agricultural supplies
88	Live animals
89	Subsistence
91	Fuels, lubricants, oils, and waxes
93	Nonmetallic fabricated materials
94	Nonmetallic crude materials
95	Metal bars, sheets, and shapes
96	Ores, minerals, and their primary products
99	Miscellaneous

Introducing a New Item

The Federal Government, especially DoD, buys many different products. If your firm makes a product, there is a good chance that DoD already buys something like it. If so, the advice in the following section may help you find a purchaser. You may feel, however, that your product is unique. How then should you proceed?

The Federal catalog system, described above, is based on the idea of one NSN for any one item, and the assignment of each particular class of product to a single manager. To sell your item, you need to get it assigned an NSN. The first step is for you to find out what the Government already buys. You should obtain the specifications (and standards, if applicable) for products similar to yours. Any Government small business specialist can help you review the indexes mentioned above under "Types of Specifications." You should study the differences between your item and those now in the system. You can then get in touch with the organization that writes specifications for items such as yours. You can try to persuade it to modify the specification so that your product will be acceptable under an existing NSN, or to write a new specification to cover your product. Before doing this, the organization will need to determine the potential need for the product; you may be able to help at this point.

If your new item has been accepted in the commercial marketplace but does not yet have an NSN, you may be able to arrange for it to be put on a New Item Introductory Schedule. The General Services Administration (GSA) uses that process when various Federal agencies might be interested in the new product. Their World Wide Web address is: http://www.gsa.gov/

DoD Central Contractor Registration (CCR)
On October 1, 1996, the DoD implemented the capability for contractors to register in the CCR. The DoD has determined the CCR acquisition reform initiative will assist the Department in complying with recent legislation. CCR is the single DoD registration for contractors who conduct business or who are interested in conducting business with the Department. CCR allows Federal Government contractors to provide basic information on business capabilities, and financial information one time to the government.

DoD requires contractors to register in the Federal CCR in order to obtain future solicitation awards, or payments, for goods or services provided to the DoD. For information on "Free" registration contact:

Department of Defense
Electronic Commerce Information Center
1-800-334-3414 or visit Website at: http://www.acq.osd.mil/

Government Purchase Card
The Government Purchase Card is playing a key role in the drive to streamline the Federal Acquisition Process. It provides DoD Military and Civilian personnel with the authority to purchase their own small dollar ($2,500 and less) commercial supplies and services without having to go through a contracting office. What this means is that DoD personnel can satisfy their needs faster and more economically. Savings are being found with commercial vendors as well. When the card is used for purchasing, the vendor does not have to submit invoices and wait the usual 30 days for payment. With the

purchase card, vendors are paid within 72 hours. If your company already accepts credit cards, transaction procedures are identical. If your company does not currently accept credit cards, contact your local bank or financial institution. Once your application is complete, it takes about 21 days to begin accepting transactions.

As with all credit card transactions, there is a fee assessed to the merchant when cards are used. Cost is based on the volume of your card business and the average size of your transactions. Be sure to shop around for the lowest fee possible - rates are competitive.

SOURCES OF INFORMATION ON DEFENSE PROCUREMENT

If you want to do business with DoD, you should determine whether there is a DoD market for your products or services. Parts 2, 3, and 4 of this special report identify the products and services used by DoD and the offices that buy them. A review of these parts of this special report will indicate whether there is a potential market for your products or services within DoD. Note that while DoD purchases products and services to meet specific operational or inventory level requirements, the timing of the purchases depends on the Federal Government's budget process. In addition to the existence of the potential need and the specific purchase office you may sell to, you need to know when your products or services will be purchased.

Small Business Advisors
Every DoD purchasing office has at least one small business specialist. These specialists can provide information about contracting and subcontracting opportunities with that office and at other DoD purchasing offices. The telephone number provided for each activity listed in this special report is that of this specialist. In addition, DoD publishes a directory of its small business specialists listing, by name, location, and phone number, every such specialist in DoD.

Solicitation Mailing Lists
Every DoD purchasing activity maintains lists of prospective suppliers that have indicated their desire to sell their products or services to that activity. These solicitation mailing lists (SMLs) are the key to obtaining maximum opportunities to compete for DoD requirements. When your name is placed on an SML, most solicitations for that product or service will automatically be issued to you. When an SML is extremely long, the purchasing activity may use only a portion of it for any one solicitation. In such situations, a prorata number of small businesses will be included in the solicitation. If you do not respond, either by an offer or by a request for retention on the list, to each solicitation you receive, your name may be deleted from the SML. Detailed instructions for getting listed in SMLs are provided below, in the section entitled "Making Your Capabilities Known." Note: SMLs may not be used when electronic commerce methods are used which transmit solicitation or presolicitation notices automatically to all interested sources participating in electronic contracting with the purchasing activity.

Bid Boards

Every DoD purchasing activity maintains, in a public place, a bulletin board on which is displayed a notice or copy of each proposed contract action between $10,000 to $25,000. If it is impractical to post a copy of the proposed action, the bulletin board notice describes the action and tells where a copy may be examined. The action or notice is posted on the bid board on the date the solicitation is issued and is kept there for at least 10 days or until after quotations have opened, whichever is later.

Commerce Business Daily

Another way to learn of proposed purchases is through the Commerce Business Daily (CBD). This paper, published every working day by the Department of Commerce, lists virtually every proposed DoD procurement estimated to exceed $25,000. It lists major DoD prime contract awards that have potential subcontracting opportunities. It also contains information about DoD needs for R&D efforts in fields in which unsolicited proposals may be appropriate. Each issue of the CBD contains large amounts of information in highly condensed form. Explanatory notes are included only in the Monday edition. It may be advisable to review a copy before subscribing; only you can determine its utility for your particular needs. The CBD is available for inspection at each DoD purchasing and contract administration activity and at all field offices of the SBA, the Department of Commerce, and GSA, as well as some local chambers of commerce and libraries. (http://www.acq.osd.mil/sadbu).

Small Business Innovation Research Program (SBIR) and Small Business Technology Transfer (STTR) Programs

The purpose of DoD's SBIR and STTR programs is to harness the innovative talents of our nation's small technology companies for the benefit of the U.S. military and the U.S. economy.

DoD's SBIR program funds early-stage R&D projects at small technology companies -- projects which serve a DoD need and have the potential for commercialization in private sector and/or military markets. The program, funded at roughly $530 million per year, is part of a larger ($1.1 billion) federal SBIR program administered by ten federal agencies. (For information on the ten-agency federal SBIR program, call the Small Business Administration at (202) 205-6450, or see the SBA's Home Page, at: (http://www.sbaonline.sba.gov/.)

As part of its SBIR program, the DoD issues an SBIR research solicitation twice a year, describing its R&D needs and inviting R&D proposals from small companies. Companies apply first for a six-month phase I award of up to $100,000 to test the scientific, technical, and commercial merit and feasibility of a particular concept. If phase I proves successful, the company may be invited to apply for a two-year phase II award of up to $750,000 to further develop the concept, usually to the prototype stage. Proposals are judged competitively on the basis of scientific, technical, and commercial merit. Following completion of phase II, small companies are expected to obtain funding from the private sector and/or non-SBIR government sources to develop the concept into a product for sale in private sector and/or military markets.

In 1992, Congress established the STTR pilot program. STTR is similar in structure to SBIR but funds *cooperative* R&D projects involving a small business and a university, federally-funded R&D center, or nonprofit research institution. DoD's STTR program, is part of a larger ($60 million) federal STTR program administered by five federal agencies. (For information on the five-agency federal STTR program, call the Small Business Administration at (202) 205-6450, or see the SBA's SBIR/STTR Home Page, at http://www.sbaonline.sba.gov/sbir/). DoD issues one STTR research solicitation each year.

To obtain hard copies of current and future DoD SBIR and STTR solicitations, place your name and address on the SBIR/STTR mailing list by calling 800/382-4634. You can also access each solicitation electronically on the DoD SBIR/STTR Home Page (http://www.acq.osd.mil/sadbu/sbir), starting four to six weeks before the official opening date (i.e., before October 1 or June 1 for SBIR, and before December 1 for STTR).

If you have general questions about the DoD SBIR or STTR programs, please call the DoD SBIR/STTR Help Desk at 800/382-4634.

Procurement Technical Assistance (PTA) Cooperative Agreement Program
The PTA Program is a Congressionally authorized DoD initiative designed to establish a network of assistance offices for business entities seeking to market their goods and/or services to federal, state and local governments. The Defense Logistics Agency awards cost sharing cooperative agreements for this purpose. Recipients of these agreements are state and local governments, private nonprofit and tribal organizations and Indian economic enterprises. Recipients provide technical expertise in such areas as identifying bid opportunities through bid matching, bid and proposal preparation, preaward surveys, quality assurance and accounting systems. Business firms interested in marketing their products and/or services to the federal, state and local governments should contact these centers.

More information regarding this Program and a current list of cooperative agreement recipients are available from the Program Manager, Small and Disadvantaged Business Utilization, Headquarters, Defense Logistics Agency, 8725 John J. Kingman Road, Suite 2533, Room 1127, Fort Belvoir, VA 22060-6221, telephone (703) 767-1650. You may also visit the DLA PTA page at http://www.dla.mil/db/procurem.htm, or the DLA Small Business Page, at http://www.dla.mil/.

SUBCONTRACTING OPPORTUNITIES

Subcontracting offers small business firms an important means of participating in DoD purchasing; particularly, if your capabilities are such that prime contracts are not within your reach. Some of the most significant factors to consider in deciding whether you want to be a subcontractor to a DoD prime contractor are listed below:

- Production for DoD is often intricate and exacting. Subcontractors frequently have to work to very close tolerances, under precise specifications, and with tight delivery schedules.
- Subcontractors have no contractual relationship with the Government.
- The prime contractor will need to know as much about your organization and its ability to perform the work as is needed to make the determination of responsibility described previously.

If you are interested in pursuing DoD subcontracting opportunities, there are two major sources of information. One is the CBD, which lists awards of contracts in excess of $100,000 that provide subcontracting opportunities. The other stems from DoD's efforts to maximize small business subcontracting opportunities. Large business firms receiving DoD construction contracts in excess of $1,000,000 or other contracts in excess of $500,000 offering subcontracting possibilities are required to establish plans for subcontracting to small and small disadvantaged business. These contractors must designate a small business liaison officer to administer these plans. DoD annually publishes Subcontracting Opportunities with DoD Major Prime Contractors, which lists all these prime contractors, their product lines, and the names and telephones numbers of their small business liaison officers. This directory is a major source of leads to subcontracting opportunities with DoD prime contractors and is available on the OSD SADBU website (http://www.acq.osd.mil/sadbu) under publications.

MAKING YOUR CAPABILITIES KNOWN

If you find a potential market between DoD's needs and your firm's capabilities, you need to make these capabilities known. The ways to do this vary depending on the nature of your business. The suggestions provided here are in addition to your normal marketing procedures.

Getting on Solicitation Mailing Lists (SML)
The most common way to match your capabilities with the potential DoD market is to have your firm listed on the appropriate SMLs of those activities you hope to contract with for your products or services. To accomplish this, you should get advice from the small business specialists at your selected purchasing activities. Virtually every DoD purchasing activity uses Standard Form 129, Solicitation Mailing List Application. However, this basic document almost always needs to be supplemented by other documents or listings useful only in the individual activity. You must submit a separate application to each activity you hope to sell to. Note that each activity may have slightly different instructions for this information. To ensure that your capabilities will be made known at each purchasing activity, be sure you follow the specific procedures and suggestions of that activity.

The small business specialist at any activity will furnish the forms free and will help you with their preparation. Purchasing activities identify source lists by means of the FSCs. This means you should know the FSC codes applicable to your products and services and enter them on your SML applications. Note that Part 2 of this special report identifies the FSCs for products purchased by major military purchasing offices.

You will expedite the processing of your SML application if you also complete and submit a DD Form 2051, Request for Assignment of a Commercial and Government Entity (CAGE) Code. The CAGE code is a five position alpha numeric identifier assigned by the Defense Logistics Services Center, Battle Creek, Michigan. The code identifies the contractor plant or establishment as a unique entity. CAGE numbers are used by many purchasing activities to identify the firms with which they do business.

To obtain a CAGE contractors can now submit DD Form 2051 (request for CAGE Code) on-line. The Defense Logistics Services Center has a bulletin board for CAGE Code assignment and maintenance. On-line submission allows a 3 to 5 days turn around. Go to: http://www.dlis.dla.mil/cageserv.asp for more information.

Research and Development Brochures

If you are interested mainly in obtaining R&D contracts, you should consider preparing an R&D brochure covering your organization and its capabilities. Obtaining an R&D contract requires a selling job to the technical personnel of the appropriate DoD purchasing activity. Experienced firms report that a well-thought-out brochure quickly establishes their basic qualifications and field of endeavor. At a minimum, an R&D brochure should identify work you have done or are doing, the type of work for which you are specially qualified, and the names and qualifications of key scientific and primary technical personnel on your staff or available to you, and should describe your facilities and equipment. Note any Government prime or subcontract work you may have done, together with any DoD or other Government agency security clearance you may have. When you contact a DoD purchasing office, you should present your brochure to both the contracting and the technical personnel.

Unsolicited Proposals

Sometimes you can create your own contracting opportunities by submitting unsolicited proposals to perform R&D work or to introduce a new or improved item that may be of interest to DoD. You can learn about DoD R&D needs from advance notices in the CBD. Informal contacts with agency personnel are also a good means of obtaining this information. To be considered, an unsolicited proposal must offer a unique and innovative concept to the Government. Your proposal should contain an abstract of the proposed effort, the method of approach, and the extent of the effort. It should also include a proposed price or estimated cost. If it includes any proprietary data you wish to protect against disclosure to third parties, you should clearly mark such data with a restrictive legend

Special Procedures for Architect-Engineer Firms

Architect-engineer (A&E) services are contracted for under a special procedure established by law. It does not involve submission of bids, and SMLs are not maintained for A&E services. The selection of A&E firms for DoD contracts is based upon the professional qualifications necessary for satisfactory performance of the services required.

Selection is subject to the following criteria:

- Professional qualifications necessary for satisfactory performance of required services.
- Specialized experience and technical competence in the type of work required.
- Capability to accomplish the work in the required time.
- Past performance on contracts (Government or commercial) in terms of cost control, quality of work, and compliance with performance schedules.
- Location of the firm in the general geographical area of the project and knowledge of the locality of the project.
- Volume of work previously awarded by DoD to the firm (the object is to effect equitable distribution of work among qualified A&E firms).

Firms wishing to be considered for A&E contracts should send their qualifications to the activities responsible for the geographic area(s) in which the firm desires to work. These qualifications must be submitted by filing Standard Form 254, Architect-Engineer and Related Services Questionnaire, with the selected activities. In response to a specific project announcement, interested firms should submit Standard Form 255, Architect-Engineer and Related Services Questionnaire for Specific Project. Additional forms may be obtained from any military or other Federal Government construction office.

All requirements for A&E services are publicly announced. When a contract is not expected to exceed $10,000, an agency evaluation board or the chairperson of such a board will review the current data files on eligible firms (i.e., Standard Forms 254, Architect-Engineer and Related Services Questionnaire, and 255, Architect-Engineer and Related Services Questionnaire for Special Project, and performance reports) and evaluate those firms in accordance with the above criteria. A designated individual in the agency reviews this evaluation and establishes a listing, in order of preference, of at least three firms considered most highly qualified to perform the work. This list of "selected firms" is then provided to the contracting officer, who obtains a proposal from and negotiates with the most preferred firm. If a mutually satisfactory contract cannot be negotiated, the contracting officer so notifies that firm and proceeds to the next most preferred firm. For contracts expected to exceed $10,000, the agency's evaluation board must hold discussions with at least three of the most highly qualified firms regarding concepts and the relative utility of alternative methods of furnishing the required services.

Contracts estimated to cost under $85,000 are generally reserved for small business firms.

For more detailed information on A&E procedures, see Subpart 36.6 of the FAR.

Local Purchases

Virtually all military installations are authorized to make local purchases and to contract for various services. Typically, local purchases are made under the following conditions:

- The purchase is small, usually $100,000 or less.
- The items to be purchased are not centrally procured or stocked.
- The items are to be consumed locally.
- The products or services are required for maintenance and repair of buildings of the installation or for equipment stored at the installation.

Examples of products and services purchased locally are office supplies, automotive spare parts, tools and equipment, some perishable food items for troop meals, laundry and dry cleaning, refuse collection, job-lot printing, and repair and maintenance.

For the most part, local purchases are made from sources near the purchasing installation. While proposed local purchases in excess of $25,000 will be published in the CBD, most of those for lesser amounts will not. The marketing strategy for firms whose products and services correspond to the typical local purchase situation should be directed toward the requirements of military installations within their geographic area.

Electronic Commerce (EC) and Electronic Data Interchange (EDI)

Background - The DoD is rapidly moving to an electronic environment in the conduct of business transactions with private industry. The bulk of DoD business transactions associated with procurement and contract administration are increasing being electronically integrated. Business firms, both large and small, interested in doing business with the DoD will need to make appropriate adjustments to maintain a sound business relationship with the DoD.

EC & EDI - Consider EC as the conduct of business transactions (including the supporting functions of administration, finance, logistics, procurement, and transportation) between the DoD and private industry, using an integrated automated information environment. Consider EDI as the computer-to-computer exchange of routine business information using standard electronic formats. Translation software aids in that exchange by converting data extracted from your application data base into a standard EDI format for transmission to one or more trading partners. It also converts EDI-formatted data received from those trading partners into a file format your application system recognizes. Ultimately, the data is processed and written to your data base.

Benefits of Using EC/EDI - EC/EDI uses technology resources readily available commercially. Some firms currently possess the necessary technology and, accordingly, will not need to invest in capital resources. The generally acknowledged benefits of using EC/EDI are: improved business opportunities; improved record-keeping, fewer mistakes, reduced processing delays, less reliance on human interpretation of data; greater competition and reduced prices; reduced order time; savings from reduced inventories, elimination of lost documents; and better information for management decision-making.

Electronic Commerce Information Center (ECIC)
The ECIC was formally established in November 1994 to provide all necessary information to current and potential contractors and governmental activities on how to conduct business electronically with the DoD and other federal agencies. The ECIC can be reached by phone from 8AM to 8PM EST at 1-800-EDI-3414 or (703)681-0211, by facsimile at (703) 275-5691, or by mail at the following address: Electronic Commerce Office Information Center, 7676 Old Springhouse Road, McLean, VA 22102. The World Web Website address is: http://www.acq.osd.mil/ec.

Chapter 2:

TYPES OF PRODUCTS AND SERVICES BOUGHT BY MAJOR MILITARY PURCHASING OFFICES

The first part of this section lists the major military purchasing offices of the Army, Navy, Air Force, and Defense Logistics Agency (DLA). The accompanying description summarizes the procurement responsibilities of each of these offices. This list will help you determine which major purchasing offices offer sales opportunities for your firm. The telephone numbers are those of the small business specialists.

The second section of this part lists the products and services purchased by the major military purchasing offices. It will be easier to locate sales opportunities for specific items from this list. These items are listed in the numerical sequence of their FSC codes. Once you have located the product or service in which you are interested, note the alphanumeric designators that appear after it. These designators refer back to the major purchasing offices. For example, look at the classification "FSC 1560 Airframe Components, A-3, D-3" in the listings of products and services. After this classification appear "A-3 and D-3." By turning to the list of major purchasing offices and locating these designators, you will find that Airframe Components are purchased by U.S. Army Aviation and Missile Command, Redstone Arsenal, AL and Defense Supply Center, Richmond, VA.

For each product or service, the FSC list refers to the major buying offices. Other offices may also buy the listed items, but less frequently. You may form your own opinion on the basis of the brief descriptions furnished for each of the major purchasing offices listed. If your product or service can be acquired under the simplified acquisition procedures, you should ensure that those potential buyers geographically closest to you are aware of your desire to supply their needs. A geographical listing of all military purchasing offices is contained in the booklet entitled Small Business Specialists.

Suppose, for example, that your product is used by data processing groups. The listing suggests "General Purchase" for all the subcodes of group 70. This means that contracts for ADP equipment and support are awarded not only by major buying offices but by others, too. Your marketing effort should, therefore, focus not only on the major offices, but on all offices conveniently located to you; you can find a geographic listing of purchase offices in Small Business Specialists.

Services tend to be acquired locally. You should look in the listing arranged by FSC codes, showing the major buying offices that make significant amounts of awards for each category of service. But, for most services, you should arrange to get on the appropriate SMLs of the DoD buying offices in your region.

Remember, you are not selling your product! You are letting the Government's buyer know about you. The Government will not usually be able to respond immediately. It may be as much as a year after you express your interest before you routinely receive solicitations.

MAJOR MILITARY PURCHASING OFFICES
LISTED BY DOD COMPONENT

Major Army Buying Offices

U. S. Army Industrial Operations Command
ATTN: AMSIO-SB
Rock Island, IL 61299-6000
(309) 782-7302

Principal interests: Ammunition, fuses, projectile assemblies, mortars; ammunition destruction; nuclear and nonnuclear munitions; rocket and missile warhead sections; demolition munitions; mines, bombs, grenades; and pyrotechnic boosters.

U. S. Army Chemical Biological Defense Command
AMSCB-SBA(A)
Aberdeen Proving Ground, MD 21010-5423
(410) 671-3136

Principal Interests: Research, concept exploration, demonstration and validation, engineering manufacturing development and internal production of chemical defense system, obscuring smoke and aerosol systems and flame weapons, chemical material destruction (stockpile/nonstockpile)

U. S. Army Aviation and Missile Command
AMSAM-SB
Redstone Arsenal, AL 35898-5150
(205) 876-5441

Principal Interests: Army aircraft, equipment, and supplies; development of turbine engines and new helicopter systems. Free rockets, guided missiles, ballistic missiles, targets, air defense, fire control coordination equipment, related special-purpose and multisystem test equipment, missile launching and ground support equipment, and metrology and calibration equipment.

U. S. Army Communications and Electronics
Command, AMSEL-SB
Fort Monmouth, NJ 07703-5005
(908) 532-4511

Principal interests: Communications-electronics systems and subsystems and related equipment for command, control and communications; countermine and tactical sensor equipment.

U. S. Army Communications and Electronics
Command Acquisition Center-Combat Support
Center, AMSEL-CB
Fort Huachuca, AZ 85613-5300
(520) 538-7870

Principal Interests: Equipment and systems to support the Army's total information needs, including communications, data processing, and multi-command management information systems.

U. S. Army Communications and Electronics
Command Acquisition Center-Washington
Operations Office
2461 Eisenhower Avenue, Hoffman 1 Building
Alexandria, Virginia 22331-0700
(703) 325-5793

Principal interests: Automated information hardware, software, services, maintenance, and systems.

U. S. Army Research Laboratory
ATTN: AMSRL-SB
2800 Powder Mill Road
Adelphia, MD 20783-1197
(301) 394-3692

Principal Interests: Nuclear survivability, lethality, radar, signal sensors, signatures, information processing; electronic surveillance systems; high-power microwave and acoustic technology, materials, digitization of battlefield, MANTECH, advanced computing.

U. S. Army Tank-automotive and Armaments Command
AMSTA-CS-CB
Warren, MI 48397-5000
(810) 574-5388

Principal interests: Ground vehicles (tanks, infantry fighting vehicles, trucks and trailers, construction and material handling vehicles); vehicle components and supplies (e.g., power train components, electronic assemblies, armor, tires, special purpose kits); combat engineering equipment (e.g., bridges); railway cars; watercraft; fuel and water tanks; and research and development services (product development/ improvement, testing and analysis, technical support for fielded systems).

U. S. Army Armament and Chemical Acquisition and Logistics Activity
AMSTA-AC-SB
Rock Island, IL 61299-7630
(309) 782-6709

Principal Interests: Armament systems (artillery, small arms, fire control equipment); armament components and supplies (e.g., optical equipment, electronic assemblies); and chemical, nuclear and biological protection equipment.

U. S. Army Armament Research,
Development and Engineering Center
AMSTA-AR-SB
Picatinny Arsenal, NJ 07806-5000
(201) 724-4106

Principal interests: Product development/improvement of munitions, weaponry, and fire control systems; testing and analysis; and technical support for fielded armament systems.

Department of the Army
Defense Supply Service-Washington
5200 Army Pentagon
Washington, D. C. 20310-5200
(703) 697-6024

Principal interests: Supplies, materials, and equipment; research; contractual services; studies and analytical support services; machine rental, repair, and maintenance services; and other related services for DoD agencies located in or near Washington, D. C.

Military Traffic Management Command
5611 Columbia Pike, ATTN: MTAQ-S
Falls Church, VA 22041-5050
(703) 681-3515

Principal interests: Stevedoring and related terminal services; transportation and storage of personal property, including household goods; commercial travel services; federal information processing services, and transportation of personnel.

Military Traffic Management Command,
Eastern Area Acquisition Office
ATTN: MTELO-CO, Building 42
Bayonne Military Ocean Terminal, Room 705A
Bayonne, NJ 07002-5302
(201) 823-6509

Principal interests: Repair and maintenance services for the Defense Freight Railway Interchange Fleet; processing privately-owned vehicles; terminal support supplies and services, and other services such as guard, trucking, towing, janitorial, refuse collection, and minor construction and repair.

Military Traffic Management Command
Western Area Acquisition Office
MTWLO-CO, Oakland Army Base
Oakland, CA 94626-5000
(510) 466-2703

Principal interests: Container freight stuffing and unstuffing, processing privately-owned vehicles; reefer cargo services, base maintenance services, and minor construction and repair.

U. S. Army Medical Research & Materiel Command
MCMR-AAA
820 Chandler Street
Fort Detrick, MD 21702-5014
(301) 619-2471

Principal interests: Basic and applies medical research and product development. Medical laboratory and logistical support services, supplies, equipment, and telecommunications.

U. S. Army Medical Commands
Principal interests: Medical supplies and equipment, direct health care professionals.
Fitzsimons Army Medical Center
MCHG-DC
Aurora, CO 80045-5000
(303) 361-8488

Walter Reed Army Medical Center
MCHL-Z
Washington, D. C. 20307-5000
(202) 782-1255

Dwight D. Eisenhower Army Medical Center
MCAA-SE
Fort Gordon, GA 30905-5650
(706) 787-6793

Tripler Army Medical Center
MCAA-PC
Honolulu, HI 96819
(808) 433-3503

Brooke Army Medical Center
MCAA-C
Fort Sam Houston, TX 78234-6039
(210) 221-9088

William Beaumont Army Medical Center
MCAA-SW
El Paso, TX 79920-5001
(915) 569-2815

Madigan Army Medical Center
MCAA-NW
Tacoma, WA 94831-5021
(206) 698-4914

U. S. Army Depots

Principal interests: Overhaul, rebuild, and modify munitions, weapon systems, helicopters, and communication equipment.

Anniston Army Depot
SIOAN-DOC
Anniston, AL 36201-5003
(205) 235-4258

Bluegrass Army Depot
SIOBG-PO
Richmond, KY 40475-5115
(606) 625-6866

Corpus Christi Army Depot
SIOCC-C
Corpus Christi, TX 78419-6170
(512) 939-3913

Letterkenny Army Depot
SIOLE-P
Chambersburg, PA 17201-4150
(717) 267-9007

Red River Army Depot
SIORR-P
Texarkana, TX 75507-5000
(903) 334-3989

Sierra Army Depot
SIOSI-CONT
Herlong, CA 96113-5009
(916) 827-4836

Tobyhanna Army Depot
SIOTY-K
Tobyhanna, PA 18466-5045
(717) 895-7232
Tooele Army Depot

SIOTE-CO
Tooele, UT 84074-5020
(801) 833-2616

U. S. Army Corps of Engineers
20 Massachusetts Avenue, N. W.
Washington, D. C. 20314-1000
(202) 761-0725

Principal interests: Designs and manages the construction of military facilities for the Army and Air Force. Provides design and construction management support for other DOD and Federal agencies. Plans, designs, builds and operates water resources and other civil works projects. Provides research and development services for both military and civil works projects and for other agencies on a reimbursable basis..

Other Army Commands

Principal interests: Supplies and services in support of each installation such as: office supplies/services, grounds maintenance, ADP maintenance and repair, laundry services, refuse collection, food services, printing, education and training services, minor construction, building maintenance and repair, and automotive spare parts.

U. S. Army Training & Doctrine Command
ATCS-B
Fort Monroe, VA 23651-5000
(757) 727-3291

US Army Forces Command
AFCS-SB
Fort McPherson, GA 30330-6000
(404) 464-6223

National Guard Bureau
NGB-SADBU
Falls Church, VA 22041-3201
(703) 681-0655

US Army Military District of Washington
ANPC-SB
Fort Leslie J. McNair
Washington, D. C. 20319-5058
(202) 685-1990

US Army, Pacific
APAM
Fort Shafter, HI 96858-5100
(808) 438-6530

Major Navy Buying Offices

Headquarters U.S. Marine Corp
Code L-2
2 Navy Annex
Washington, DC 20380-1775
(703) 696-1022

Principal interests: Electronics equipment, specialized vehicles, and equipment peculiar to the Marine Corps.

Marine Corps Systems Command
Code SBS ext. 236
2033 Barnett Avenue, Suite 315
Quantico, VA 22134-5010
(703) 784-5822

Principal interest: Research, development and acquisition of equipment, information systems, training systems and weapon systems to satisfy approved material requirements of the Marine Corps.

Military Sealift Command
Washington Navy Yard, Bldg-210,
Code NOOB, Room 419
901 M. Street, SE
Washington, DC 20398-5100
(202) 685-5025

Principal interests: Ocean shipping services to maintain strategic sealift, support of fleet units worldwide, and meeting special transportation needs of DoD sponsors for research, cable laying and repair, and special missions; movement of material, petroleum, oil, and lubricants, and personnel using U.S.-flag vessels; repair of oceangoing noncombatant ships.

Office of Naval Research
Code 00SB
800 North Quincy Street, Rm 704
Arlington, VA 22217-5660
(703) 696-4605

Principal interests: Studies in the areas of mathematical and physical sciences, environmental sciences, engineering sciences, life sciences, and technology projects.

Naval Research Laboratory
Code 3204
Building 222, Room 115
4555 Overlook Ave., SW
Washington, D.C. 20375-5326
(202) 767-6263

Principal interests: Scientific research and advanced technology development for new and improved materials, equipment, techniques, systems and related operational procedures for the Navy. Fields of interest include space science and systems; environmental sciences; plasma physics; acoustics; radar; electronic warfare; marine technology; chemistry; materials; optical and radiation sciences; electronics and information technology.

Strategic Systems Program
Code, SP-01G1
1931 Jefferson Davis Highway
Arlington, VA 22241-5362
(703) 607-0217

Principal interests: Fleet ballistic missiles.

Naval Air Systems Command
Building 441
21983 Bundy Road, Unit 8
Patuxent River, MD 20670
(301) 757-9044

Principal interests: Navy and Marine Corps aircraft systems; air-launched weapons systems and subsystems; airborne electronics systems; air-launched underwater sound systems; airborne pyrotechnics; astronautics and spacecraft systems; airborne mine countermeasures equipment (except for explosives, explosive components, and fusing); aeronautical drones and towed target systems, including related ground control equipment and launch and control aircraft; meteorological equipment; overhaul and modification of all Naval aircraft/engines; operation and maintenance of weapons training ranges.

Naval Air Warfare Center
Aircraft Division
Code 29.S South, Building 129
Lakehurst, NJ 08053-5082
(908) 323-2812

Principal interests: Launching, guidance, and recovery of Navy and Marine Corps aircraft in connection with test and evaluation; test design; stress analysis; structures; environmental simulation; design evaluation; aeronautical design; hydraulics; computer sciences; metallurgy; synthetic materials; electrical systems; mechanical systems and electronics; industrial engineering; optics; propulsion systems; acoustics; corrosion control; cryogenics; and control techniques. Procurements also include ground support equipment such as handling and servicing; armament support; avionics, propulsion, and mechanical devices; and medium and heavy machine shop assemblies and components.

Naval Air Warfare Center
Aircraft Division, Code 20C00W
Contracts Building 588, Suite 2
22347 Cedar Point Road, Unit 6
Patuxent River, MD 20670-1161
(301) 342-7567 Ext. 103

Principal interests: Development of aircraft systems and their components; also antisubmarine warfare command systems and related equipment.

Naval Air Warfare Center
Weapons Division, Code 00K000D
One Administration Circle
China Lake, CA 93555-6001
(760) 939-2712

Principal interests: Air warfare systems (except antisubmarine warfare systems) and missile weapons systems including propulsion, warheads, fuses, avionics and fire control, and guidance; and the national range/facility for parachute test and evaluation.

Naval Air Warfare Center
Training Systems Division
Code 86D1/27B
12350 Research Parkway
Orlando, FL 32826-3224
(407) 380-8253

Principal interests: Training aids, devices, equipment, and material for the Navy,
Marine Corps, and other DoD activities.

Space and Naval Warfare Systems Command
Code SPA-OOK
4301 Pacific Highway
San Diego, CA 92110-3127
(619)524-7701

Principal interests: Shore (ground) electronics; shipboard communications IFF, ECM,
radio-navigation; fixed underwater surveillance systems; navigation aids; landing aids
and air traffic control aids, except airborne communications via satellite and space
surveillance systems; shore-based strategic data systems; communication data-link
systems; radial equipment; special communications for fleet ballistic missile systems;
standardized telemetry equipment and components; cryptographic equipment;
expeditionary and amphibious electronic equipment; multiplatform electronic systems
not otherwise assigned; antenna design and integration.

Space and Navy Warfare System Center
RDT&E Division, Code 02202
53570 Silvergate Avenue
San Diego, CA 92152-5113
(619) 553-4326

Principal interests: New developments in command, control, and communications,
electronic warfare, ocean surveillance, antisubmarine warfare weapon systems,
submarine arctic warfare, ocean science, ocean engineering, biosystems research, and
related technologies. Purchases include computer software and systems engineering
services, computer equipment, electronic test instruments, and miscellaneous support
equipment and services.

Space and Navy Warfare System Center
Code OAL
P.O. Box
North Charleston, SC 29419-9022
(803) 974-5115

Principal interests: Sensors, video teleconferencing, image processing, air traffic control, meteorology, navigation, physical and computer security, command and control, communications, and cryptologic and intelligence.

Naval Facilities Engineering Command
Code FAC-OOJ
200 Stovall Street, Room 11N59
Alexandria, VA 22332-5000
(703) 325-8549

Principal interests: Cranes; power plants; floating pile drivers; major boiler plants and electrical generators; and permanent facilities (including acquisition and disposal of real estate); design and construction projects as well as station maintenance and repair, including public utilities services.

Navy Construction
Principal interests: A&E services, construction, and major maintenance and repair of naval facilities.

Northern Division
Naval Facilities Engineering Command
Code 09J
10 Industrial Highway, M/S 82
Lester, PA 19113-2090
(610) 595-0637

Atlantic Division
Naval Facilities Engineering Command
Code 09W
1510 Gilbert Street
Norfolk, VA 23511-2699
(757) 322-8222

Southern Division
Naval Facilities Engineering Command
Code 09J, P. O. , Box 190010
2155 Eagle Drive
North Charleston, SC 29419-9010
(803) 820-5935

Southwest Division
Naval Facilities Engineering Command
Code 09J
1220 Pacific Highway
San Diego, CA 92132-5190
(619) 532-3003

Pacific Division
Naval Facilities Engineering Command
Code 09J
4262 Radford Drive
Honolulu, HI 96818
(808) 471-4577

Engineering Field Activity, Chesapeake
Naval Facilities Engineering Command
Code O9J, Building 212
Washington Navy Yard
901 M Street, SE
Washington, DC 20374-2121
(202) 685-0088

Engineering Field Activity, Midwest
Naval Facilities Engineering Command Ext 105
Code 09J, Building 1A, Suite 120
2703 Sheridan Road
Great Lakes, IL 60088-5600
(847) 688-2600

Engineering Field Activity, Northwest
Naval Facilities Engineering Command
Code 09J
19917 Seventh Avenue, NE
Poulsbo, WA 98370-7570
(360) 396-0038

Engineering Field Activity, West
Naval Facilities Engineering Command
Code 09J
900 Commodore Drive
San Bruno, CA 94066-5006
(650) 244-2305

Navy Public Works Center
Acquisition Support Office
Code 40H
9742 Maryland Avenue
Norfolk, VA 23511-3095
(757) 444-8065 Ext. 3052

Navy Public Works Center
Contracting Department
Code 200
Pearl Harbor, HI 96860-5470
(808) 471-9997

Navy Public Works Center
Code 200D, Suite 1, Box 368113
2730 McKean Street
San Diego, CA 92136-5294
(619) 556-6352

Naval Construction Battalion Center
Code 10G/27G, Bldg 41
1000 23rd Avenue
Port Hueneme, CA 93043-4301
(805) 982-5066

Naval Sea Systems Command
Code SEA-00K
2531 Jefferson Davis Highway
Arlington, VA 22242-5160
(703) 602-1964

Principal interests: Shipboard weapons systems and components, explosives and propellants, and related actuating technology. Ship systems design and integration including construction, overhaul, modernization, and conversion; propulsion; auxiliary power generating and distribution; navigational equipment; habitability and environment control features; rescue and salvage systems; ship maintenance and support; degaussing; and shipboard minesweeping equipment, including R&D needs for these items.

Naval Surface Warfare Center
Crane Division
Code SB
300 Highway 121, Building 221A
Crane, IN 47522-5001
(812) 854-1542

Principal interests: Shipboard weapons systems and assigned ordnance items.

Naval Surface Warfare Center
Indian Head Division
Code SB
101 Strauss Avenue
Indian Head, MD 20640-5035
(301) 743-6604

Principal interests: Chemicals, igniters, metal parts, and components for rocket engines; electronic weapon system simulators and components; and cartridges, cartridge-actuated devices, and propulsive components for aircrew escape systems. Includes all related engineering tasks for fleet support and test.

Naval Surface Warfare Center
Port Hueneme Division
Code 00B, Building 5
4363 Missile Way
Port Hueneme, CA 93043-5007
(805) 982-0372

Principal Interests: Test and evaluation, inservice engineering, and integrated logistic support for Nay surface fleet surface and mine warfare combat systems, command and control systems F-I System interface, weapons systems and subsystems and related expendable ordnance. Engineering, production and logistic support for cruiser, destroyer, battleship and frigate combatants for the following software requirements: combat direction systems operational programs, inter-computer communications for integrated systems, Navy standard program generation system computer programs, and shore establishment computer programs.

Naval Surface Warfare Center
Dahlgren Division, Code CD2K
17320 Dahlgren Road
Dahlgren, VA 22448-5100
(540) 653-4806

Principal interests: Advanced technology developments in radar, communications, electronics, optics, chemistry, materials, plasma physics, space systems, and countermeasures.

Naval Surface Warfare Center
Carderock Division
Building 30, Code 303
9500 McArthur Blvd, Room 1
West Bethesda, MD 20817-5700
(301) 227-2871

Principal interests: Development and evaluation of systems, subsystems, and components.

Naval Undersea Warfare Center
Code 00SB Ext. 270
1176 Howell Street, Building 11
Newport, RI 02840
(401) 841-2442

Principal interests: Submarine and other underwater combat systems.

Navy Exchange Service Command
3280 Virginia Beach Boulevard
Virginia Beach, VA 23452-5724
(757)631-3582

Principal interests: Supplies for Navy exchanges, commissary stores, lodges, ships stores, and military sealift exchanges, including retail merchandise of various types; food; vending machine items; service station supplies; air conditioners; vehicles; hotel furnishings; store fixtures; and other supplies and equipment.

Supply Centers

Principal interests: Ship and marine equipment, parts, accessories, and components, and a wide array of services. Support for naval activities in the region.

Naval Supply System Command
Building 9
P.O. Box 2050
Mechanicsburg, PA 17055-0791
(717) 790-3575

Naval Inventory Control Point
Code 0062
P.O. Box 2020
5450 Carlisle Pike
Mechanicsburg, PA 17055-0788
(717) 790-6625

Naval Inventory Control Point
Code P0061, Room 2213A
700 Robbins Avenue
Philadelphia, PA 19111-4098
(215) 697-2806

Fleet and Industrial Supply Center
Code 04, Bldg W-143, Suite 600
1968 Gilbert Street
Norfolk, VA 23511-3392
(757) 443-1435

Fleet and Industrial Supply Center Norfolk
Detachment Washington
Code 0200SB, Building 200
Washington Navy Yard
901 M Street, SE
Washington, DC 20374-5014
(202) 433-2957

Fleet and Industrial Supply Center Norfolk
Detachment Philadelphia
Code 09B, Bldg 2B
700 Robbins Avenue
Philadelphia, PA 19111-5083
(215) 697-9555

Fleet and Industrial Supply Center
Code COA
937 N. Harbor Drive
San Diego, CA 92132 -5075
(619) 532-3439

Fleet and Industrial Supply Center
Puget Sound
Code 04
467 W. Street
Bremerton, WA 98314-5104
(360) 476-2812

Major Air Force Buying Offices

Oklahoma City Air Logistics Center
3001 Staff Dr, Ste 1AJ84A
Tinker AFB, OK 73145-3009
(405)739-2601

Principal interests: This center repairs, maintains, and modifies the following aircraft, missiles, and engines:
Aircraft - B-1B, B-2, B-52, C/EC/RC-135, KC/NKC/WC-135, E-3
Engines - J-33 Allison, J-57 Pratt & Whitney, J-75 Pratt & Whitney, J-79 General Electric, TF-30 Pratt & Whitney, TF-33 Pratt & Whitney, TF-41 Allison/Rolls-Royce, T-58 General Electric, T-64, General Electric, F-101 General Electric, F-107

Williams,F-108 General Electric, CFM-56 General Electric/Snecma, F-110 General Electric, F-112 Williams, F-118 General Electric

Missiles - AGM-69A, AGM-84, AGM-86B/C, AGM-129A

The operational contracting division contracts for supplies, equipment, and work necessary for the operation and maintenance of Tinker AFB.

Ogden Air Logistics Center
5975 Arsenal Road
Hill AFB, UT 84056-5802
(801)777-4143

Principles interests: This center manages, repairs or purchases 350,000 items used by a variety of weapons systems in the AF.

The following lists show the assigned systems and commodities that Ogden ALC supports as a System Program Manager and Tech Repair Center.

MANAGEMENT SYSTEMS:	COMMODITIES:
F/RF-4 Phantom	Landing Gear
F-16 Fighting Falcon	Wheels and Brakes
LGM-30 Minuteman	Photographic Equipment
MGM-118A Peacekeeper	Ammunition and Explosives
AGM-65 Maverick	
GBU-15 Laser Guided	

AIRCRAFT:	MISSILES:
F-16 Fighting Falcon	AGM-65 Maverick
C-130 Hercules	ALCM-86B Cruise Missile
	AGM-69A SRAM
	LGM-118A Peacekeeper
	LGM-30 Minuteman

OTHER:

Airmunitions	
Avionics (F-4 and F-16)	Photographic Equipment
Hydraulics/Pneudraulics	
Simulators and Training	Rocket Motors
Devices	Wheels and Brakes
Instruments	External Fuel Tanks and
Landing Gear	Pylons

The operational contracting division contracts for supplies, equipment, and work necessary for the operation and maintenance of Hill AFB.

Sacramento Air Logistics Center

5033 Roberts Ave, Ste 1
McClellan AFB, CA 95652-1326
(916)643-5209

Principles interests: This center repairs, maintains, and modifies the following aircraft, missiles, and systems:

AIRCRAFT: A-10, EF-111, F-117, and F-22
SYSTEM CODE PROGRAM
404L ATCALS
407L GTACS
414L/968H Atmospheric Early Warning
428L MEECN/GWEN
433L Weather
465L SACCS
478T TRI-TAC
484L/802L Scope Command
485L GTACSI
487L MEECN
492L/493L Radio & TV
494L Telecommunications
495L AMCC2IPS
497L Ground Based Sensor
498L MILSTAR
500L Comm PG
542N Shelters
745C MILSATCOM
806L/846L/9952 Range Threat System
SRER/SRWR Space Lift Range
GROUND GENERATORS AND GENERATOR SETS:
60KW AND 72KW Aircraft Startcarts
5, 10, 15, 30, 60, 100, 200, and 750 KW Generators
50KW and 100KW Frequency Converters
Uninterruptable Power Systems
Power Conditioning and Continuation Interface Equipment
The operational contracting division contracts for supplies, equipment, and work necessary for the operation and maintenance of McClellan AFB.

San Antonio Air Logistics Center
303 S Crickett Dr, Ste 4
Kelly AFB, TX 78241-6025
(210)925-6918

Principle interests: The following are weapon systems managed by the center. The older systems that are not in the current inventory are listed because of continuing support requirements under interservice agreements or to foreign countries under the security assistance and FMS agreements.

AIRCRAFT AND COMPONENTS:
A-37 C-119 F-20 OV-10
B-57 C-123 F-84 PC-7
C-5 C-131 F-86 T-28
C-7 C-140 F-104 T-33
C-17 CASA 212 F-106 T-37
C-46 CESSNA 152 H-43 T-38
C-47 CESSNA 172 HU-16 412A
C-54 CESSNA 206 O-1 627A
C-118 F-5 O-2
ENGINES AND COMPONENTS:
F100 T53 TFE731 R4360
F103 T55 TPE33 O-300
F117 T56 TR160 IO-360
J60 T76 R1340 O-470
J65 T400 R1830 TCAE-373
J69 T700 R2000 PT6
J85 TF34 R2800
J100 TF39 R3350
AIRBORNE AUXILIARY POWER PLANTS AND GROUND GAS TURBINES
T62 T300 GTCP30 GTCP70 GTCP105
T41 GTC85 GTCP36 GTCP85 GTCP165
The operational contracting division contracts and supplies, equipment and work necessary for the operation and maintenance of Kelly AFB.

Warner Robins Air Logistics Center
180 Page Rd
Robins AFB, GA 31098-1600
(912)926-5873

Principle interests: This center repairs, maintains, and modifies the following aircraft and missiles:

AIRCRAFT/MISSILES/DRONES DIRECTORATE

C-130 Hercules C-130
C-141 Starlifter C-141
F-15 Eagle F-15
U-2 Dragon Lady U-2 Specialized Management
H-1 Helicopter (All Models) Special Operations Forces
H-53 Helicopter (All Models) Special Operations Forces
H-60 Helicopter (All Models) Special Operations Forces
C-130 (All Special Operations
Forces Configutred AC)
Special Operations Forces
97C-141B (SOLL) Special Operations Forces
AGM-45 SHRIKE Space & Special Systems
AGM-88 HARM Space & Special Systems
AIM-7 SPARROW Space & Special Systems
AIM-9 SIDEWINDER Space & Special Systems
AIM-120 AMRAAM Space & Special Systems
BQM-34A FIREBEE Space & Special Systems
FIM-92A STINGER Space & Special Systems
MQM-107 TARGET DRONE Space & Special Systems
E-8C JOINT STARS Space & Special Systems
NAVSTAR GPS Space & Special Systems
GPS RANGE APPLICATION PROGRAM Space & Special Systems
LANTRN NAVIGATION & TARGET SET Avionics
The operational contracting division contracts for supplies, equipment, and work
necessary for the operation and maintenance of Robins AFB.

Space and Missile Systems Center (SMC/BC)
155 Discoverer Blvd, Ste 2017
Los Angeles AFB CA 90245-4692
(310)363-2855

Principle interests: The mission of SMC is to plan, program, and manage AFMC
programs to acquire space systems, subsystems, support equipment, and related
hardware and software; provide for the maintenance, construction, alteration, and
security of launch, tracking, and support facilities; conduct research, exploratory
development, and advanced development programs to support future space missions;
provide for and conduct launch and flight test and evaluation support of major DoD
programs and programs of other federal agencies; perform the functions of launch,
launch control, deployment checkout prior to turnover, and sustaining engineering;
perform on-orbit test and evaluation of systems, subsystems and components, discharge
AF responsibilities for designated AF, DoD, and international space programs; plan,
program, and acquire test facilities and other test investments required by AFMC
programs at all locations (test centers and contractor facilities); plan and provide for

security on all systems and information requiring safeguards consistent with AF and DoD security directives; provide management oversight for commercial expendable Launch Vehicle Activity; conduct launch agreement negotiations with commercial space launch operators; provide system engineering management support for selected space systems, subsystems, facilities, support equipment, and related hardware and software; support other product divisions and federal agencies with technologies derived from its subordinate laboratories.

While there are no Air Force aircraft assigned to Los Angeles AFB, the operational contracting directorate does contract for all other work necessary for the operation and maintenance of the base.

11th Contracting Squadron (11CONS/LGC)
500 Duncan Ave
Bolling AFB
Washington, DC 20332-0305
(202)767-8086

Principle interests: The mission of the 11th Contracting Squadron is to provide contracting support for supplies and services necessary to the operation of approximately 300 requiring activities in the National Capital Region. The 11th Contracting Squadron (11CONS) provides support to the Office of the Secretary of Defense, Office of the Secretary of the Air Force, HQ 11th Wing and other AF agencies within the National Capitol Region. The 11 CONS operational contracting functions are responsible for purchasing base supplies, services, construction and specialized services for ADP and studies and analysis.

Typical Item Acquisitions: ADPE, Software, Hardware, Maintenance, AF Plaques, Base Supply Support, Base Wide Grounds Maintenance, Construction and AE Services, Contractor Technical Support to AF Pentagon Elements, Historical, Personnel and Research Studies, Laundry, Dry Cleaning, Maintenance, Food and Custodial Services, Logistic Systems Research and Analysis, Military Family Housing Maintenance, O&M of Computer Modeling Systems and

Base Contracting Activities: Contracting responsibility for support of a command's mission generally is assigned to a particular base or bases within the command. Contracts awarded by the other bases assigned to the command generally are limited to the supplies and services required for the daily operation of the base. The following lists are typical of the services and items bought by all base contracting offices.

Representative Service Acquisitions: Air Conditioning, General Construction, Appliance Repair, Grounds Maintenance, Architect Engineer, Laundry and Dry Cleaning, Audio Visual, Military Family Housing Maintenance, Boiler Repairs, Refuse Collection, Custodial, Road Maintenance, Education, Roofing, Environmental Detection, Steam Line Installation & Disposal/Prevention, Swimming Pool

Maintenance, Environmental Restoration, Transient Aircraft Services, Equipment Maintenance, Transportation Services, Equipment Rental, Utility Services, Equipment Repair, Various Maintenance of ADP, Food Services, Vehicles Operation & Maintenance.

Electronic Systems Center (ESC/BC)
275 Randolph Rd
Hanscom AFB, MA 01731-2818
(617)377-4 973

Principle interests: ESC plans and manages the acquisition and related engineering development of command, control, communications, and intelligence systems, subsystems and equipment including surveillance systems, navigation systems, air traffic control and landing systems, intelligence systems, electronic physical security surveillance and intrusion detection systems and weather systems, information and management systems until transfer of responsibility to the using command or agency. Evaluates using command requirements against available technology and potential costs and recommends necessary revisions. R&D contracts are also initiated by the Geophysics Division of the AF Laboratory in the environmental, physical and engineering sciences. The Geophysics Division performs research and exploratory and advanced Development in geophysics that is essential to the enhancement of AF operational capabilities. The work pursued may be categorized generally as falling within the following functional areas: Space Physics, Ionospheric Physics, Terrestrial Science, Upper Atmospheric and Stratospheric operations, Optical/IR Backgrounds and Targets, Weather Specification and Prediction. Close liaison is maintained with AF operational elements, system development activities, and other AF laboratories, to identify research and technology needs and to accelerate the integration of scientific advances into AF technology. Geophysics Division carries out its assigned R&D mission responsibilities with in-house as well as contractual support.

While there are no AF aircraft assigned to Hanscom AFB, the operational contracting directorate does contract for all other work necessary for the operation and maintenance of the base.

Aeronautical Systems Center (ASC/BC)
2196 D Street
Wright-Patterson AFB, OH 45433-7201
(937)255-5422

Principle interests: ASC's responsibilities include design, development, and acquisition programs for aeronautical systems, cruise missiles, their components, and related government-furnished aerospace equipment including aircraft engines, airborne communication systems, aircraft navigation systems, aircraft instruments; management of engineering development and initial procurement of aeronautical reconnaissance systems, aeronautical electronic warfare systems, life support systems, chemical/biological defense systems, and simulators, including armament, operational, and communication training devices.

ASC has central contracting responsibility for a number of specialized programs including the following:

Specialized Programs and Aircraft and Reconnaissance
Contractor Engineering and Technical Services
Mechanized Material Handling Systems
AF Packaging Evaluation Agency Requirements
Automatic Data Processing Studies, Software, and Equipment
Chaplain Supplies and Equipment
Educational Services Contractual Support
Library Books and Publications

ASC provides contracting support for the National Aerospace Intelligence Center which acquires, collects, analyzes, produces, and disseminates foreign aerospace scientific and technical (S&T) intelligence and intelligence information; conducts an integrated analysis program; operates an S&T intelligence data handling system; collaborates with other organizations to improve the collection, acquisition, and utilization of foreign technology and intelligence; and develops and maintains the highest attainable level of knowledge concerning foreign aerospace technology, capabilities, and limitations.

ASC Small Business Office provides contracting support for the Joint Logistics Systems Center (JLSC) which is located at Wright-Patterson AFB. JLSC is involved in the development, operation, and enhancement of the management information systems for logistics management systems for the military services and Defense Logistics Agency.
ASC Operational Contracting organization contracts for supplies, equipment, and work necessary for the operation and maintenance of Wright-Patterson AFB.

Wright Laboratory
Directorate of R&D Contracting
c/o Aeronautical Systems Center (ASC/BC)
2196 D Street
Wright-Patterson AFB OH 45433-7201
(937)255-5422

Principle interests: This directorate provides business and contracting support for Wright Laboratory (WL). Contracts are written for requirements of the following directorates: Aero Propulsion and Power Directorate is responsible for development of airbreathing propulsion and aerospace power technology needed for future AF systems, as well as providing assistance to the "product divisions" of AFMC in acquiring new systems and in helping to resolve developmental and operation problems. Avionics

Directorate conducts R&D programs for aerospace reconnaissance, weapons delivery, electronic warfare systems, navigation, communication and avionics integration. Solid State Electronics Directorate is responsible for electronic device R&D for future AF systems needs in the areas of microelectronics, microwaves, and electro-optics. Research extends from fundamental semiconductor layer growth and device fabrication through analog and digital integrated circuits; also included is the computer-aided design software and work stations needed to pursue sample hybrid and monolithic integrated circuits. Flight Dynamics Directorate pursues AF flight vehicle technologies to support aircraft, missiles and space systems in the technical areas of structures, vehicle subsystems, flight control, aeromechanics and experimental flight vehicle testbeds.

Materials Directorate explores new materials and processes for advanced aerospace applications. Its current focus is on thermal protection materials, metallic and nonmetallic structural materials, aerospace propulsion materials, fluids and lubricants, electromagnetic and electronic materials and laser hardened materials. Manufacturing Technology Directorate focuses on process technologies and integrated manufacturing. This directorate is responsible for a new initiative which integrates design and manufacturing technologies to stimulate a new focus on design for producibility, design for quality, and design for life cycle costs. Key elements of this concurrent engineering involve development of advanced tools in computer aided design and computer aided manufacturing for analyses of design for weapon performance and low cost manufacturing. Plans and Programs Directorate is made up of cockpit integration, which involves research to advance the state of the art crew systems technologies for all classes of aerospace vehicles; and signature technology, which includes planning, formulating, and executing USAF exploratory and advanced development programs for vehicle signature reduction technology and counter low observable technology. Armament Directorate develops conventional armament technology and integrates these technologies into air vehicle platforms and other delivery platforms. The directorate provides conventional armament technology for four major thrusts that include advanced guidance, weapon flight mechanics, ordnance, and conventional strategic defense.

AF Development Test Center (AFDTC/BC)
205 West D Ave, Stuite 449
Eglin AFB, FL 32542-6863
(904)882-2843

AFDTC plans, directs, and conducts the test and evaluation of nonnuclear munitions, electronic combat, and navigation/guidance systems. Related ASC System Program Offices (SPOs) are also located here and supported by AFDTC/BC. To accomplish this mission, AFDTC manages the large land test ranges that are located on the 724 square mile Eglin complex as well as the 86,500 square miles of water ranges located in the adjacent Gulf of Mexico. Major tests on or above AFDTC's ranges cover aircraft systems, subsystems, missiles, guns, rockets, targets and drones, high-powered radar, and electronic countermeasures equipment.

AFDTC's unique assets include the Guided Weapons Evaluation Facility (GWEF), the Preflight Integration of Munitions and Electronic Systems (PRIMES),and the McKinley Climatic Laboratory, a facility capable of testing military hardware as large as aircraft in environments ranging from minus 65 to plus 165 degrees Fahrenheit with 100 mph winds, icing clouds, rain, and snow. AFDTC also is responsible for the 46th Test Group at Holloman AFB NM, with its high speed test track, two radar target scatter measurement facilities, and the Central Inertial Guidance Test Facility (CIGTF). The operational contracting division contracts for supplies, equipment, and work necessary for the operation and maintenance of Eglin AFB.

Other Major Commands

Principal interests: Base contracting support, including major data major data processing, construction, and command wide acquisition of mission-related supplies and services.

3 CONS/CC
6920 12th Street, Suite 301
Elmendorf AFB, Anchorage, AK 99506-2570
(907)552-4338

Headquarters Air Education and Training Command
550 D Street East, Rm 131
Randolph AFB, TX 78150-4425
(210)652-4840

Air Military Command
402 Scott Drive, Unit 2A2
Scott AFB, IL 62225-5308
(618)256-8725

Air Combat Command
130 Douglas Street, Suite 210
Langley AFB, VA 23665-2791
(757)764-5371

10th Air Base Wing (10 ABW/LGCP)
8110 Industrial Drive, Suite 103
USAF Academy, CO 80840-2315
(719)333-6642

Air Intelligence Agency
102 Hall Blvd., Suite 258
San Antonio, TX 78243-7030
(210)977-2453

Air Force Space Command
150 Vandenburg Street, Suite 1105
Peterson AFB, CO 80914-4350
(719)554-5324

15 CONS/CC
90 G Street Ext. 103
Hickam AFB, HI 96853-5320
(808)449-6860

Air Force Reserve
155 2nd Street
Robbins AFB, GA 31098-1635
(912)327-1611

Major Defense Logistics Agency Buying Offices

Defense Supply Center Columbus
3990 East Broad St.
Columbus, OH 43216-5000
(614) 692-3541
Toll-free:1(800) 262-3272

Principal interests: Guns, mechanisms and components; aircraft landing gear components; aircraft launching, landing, and ground handling equipment; aircraft wheel and brake systems; right-of-way construction and maintenance equipment, railroad; track materials, tractors; vehicular cab, body, and frame structural components; vehicular power transmission components; vehicular brake, steering, axle, wheel and track components; vehicular furniture and accessories; miscellaneous vehicular components; gasoline reciprocating engines and components; diesel engines and components; steam turbines and components; water turbines and water wheels and components; gasoline rotary engines and components; steam engines, reciprocating;

nonaircraft engine fuel system, electrical system, and engine cooling system, engine and oil filters; miscellaneous engine accessories, nonaircraft; torque converters and speed changers; gears, pulleys, sprockets, and transmission chain; belting, drive belts, V-belts, and accessories, ship and boat propulsion equipment.

Farm equipment; pest, disease, and frost control equipment; saddlery; earth moving and excavating equipment; earth boring and related equipment; road clearing and cleaning equipment; miscellaneous construction equipment; fire fighting equipment.

Marine lifesaving and diving equipment; compressors and vacuum pumps; power and hand pumps; centrifugal; separators and pressure and vacuum filters; industrial boilers; heat exchangers and steam condensers; industrial furnaces; air and water purification equipment; space heating equipment; fuel burning equipment units; miscellaneous plumbing, heating, and sanitation equipment; piping and tubing; noses and fittings, valves, powered; valves, nonpowered; motor vehicle maintenance and repair shop equipment; prefabricated and portable buildings; storage tanks; scaffolding equipment and concrete forms; prefabricated tower structures; and miscellaneous construction equipment.

Defense Energy Support Center
8725 John J. Kingman Road
Suite 4950, Room 4950
Fort Belvoir, VA 22060-6222
(703) 767-9400
1-(800) 523-2601

Principal interests: Petroleum products and petroleum related services for the U.S. military and U.S. Government agencies worldwide. Products include jet fuels, aviation gasoline, motor gasoline, gasohol, distillates, residuals, bulk lubricating oil, coal, crude oil for strategic petroleum reserve, natural gas and synfuels. Services include aircraft refueling, into-plane, bunkers, storage terminals, laboratory testing, and environmental assessment and remediation for Defense Fuel Supply Points.

Defense Supply Center Richmond
8000 Jefferson Davis
Richmond, VA 23297-5124
(804) 279-3617
1(800) 544-5634 (VA)

Principal interests: Laundry and dry cleaning equipment; shoe repairing equipment; industrial sewing machines and mobile textile repair shops; electric arc-welding equipment; woodworking machinery and equipment; printing; duplicating and bookbinding equipment; gas generating equipment; nonself-propelled materials-handling equipment; pallets, skids, load binder, and support sets: refrigeration equipment, fans, and air circulators; lugs, terminals, and terminal strips; electrical hardware and supplies; electrical insulators and insulating materials; contact brushes and electrodes; cable, cord, and wire assemblies for communication equipment: electrical motors and electrical control equipment; electrical generators and generator sets; distribution and power station transformers; miscellaneous electric power and distribution equipment; secondary batteries, miscellaneous alarm and signal systems; lighting fixtures and lamps; photographic supplies; chemicals and chemical specialties; pest control agents and disinfectants; food cooking, baking, and warming equipment; food preparation and serving sets, kits, and outfits; books and pamphlets, sheet and book music, and miscellaneous printed matter; drums and cans; commercial and industrial gas cylinders; bottles and jars; rubber, plastic, and glass fabricated materials; refractories and fire surfacing materials, asbestos, clay, cork, and other vegetable and mineral materials; ecclesiastical equipment, furnishings, and supplies; mortuary supplies; physical properties testing equipment; geophysical and astronomical instruments; scales and balances; drafting, surveying, and mapping instruments; and liquid and gas flow, liquid level, and mechanical motion measuring instruments, packaged petroleum products, cutting tools, industrial plant equipment. tackle blocks; shackles and slings; airframe structural components; parachutes; aerial pickup, delivery, and recovery systems; cargo tie-down equipment; cargo nets; aircraft accessories and components; rigging and rigging gear; deck machinery; marine hardware and hull items.

Defense Industrial Supply Center
700 Robbins Avenue
Philadelphia, PA 19111-5096
(215) 697-2747
Toll-free: 1(800) 831-1110

Principal interests: Bearings; chain and wire rope; fiber rope, cordage and twine; rope, cable, and chain fittings; ores and minerals; ferrous and nonferrous scrap; ferrous and nonferrous bars, sheets, and shapes; electrical wire and cable; screws, bolts, and studs; nuts and washers; nails, keys, and pins; rivets; fastening devices; packing and gasket materials; metal screening; coil, flat, and wire springs; rings; shims; spacers; miscellaneous hardware; plumbing fixtures and accessories; knobs and pointers; construction materials; film; kitchen equipment and appliances; lumber; photographic equipment and supplies.

Defense Supply Support Center
2800 South 20th St.
Philadelphia, PA 19101-8419
(215) 737-2321
Toll-free: 1(800) 523-0705

Principal interests: Men's and women's military clothing, dress and work; textile fabrics; wool tops; artificial leather; tents and tarpaulins; flags and pennants; leather and rubber footwear; hats and caps; canvas products; special-purpose clothing; underwear; hosiery; gloves; badges and insignia; luggage; individual equipment; body armor; specialized flight clothing; helmets. Drugs and biological; surgical dressing materials; surgical, dental, and optical instruments, equipment and supplies; X-ray equipment and supplies; hospital furniture, equipment, utensils, and supplies; medical sets, kits, and outfits; chemical analysis instruments; laboratory equipment and supplies; medicinal chemicals; hospital and surgical clothing. Perishable and nonperishable foods are purchased for distribution in the United States and overseas. Such purchases include meats and meat products, fresh fruits and vegetables, dehydrated items, seafood or water foods, cereals, dairy products, poultry, and other related food items. Canned, packaged, fresh, and frozen items are purchased in car-lots or less. Retort pouched foods are bought in large quantities as ration components.

DLA Administrative Support Center
Office of Contracting
8725 John J. Kingman Road
Suite 0119, Room 1134
Fort Belvoir, VA 22060-6220
(703) 767-1161

Principle Interests: Centralized contracting of Federal Information Processing (FIP) Resources (ADP, Computer and Telecommunications products and services) at DLA HQ for all DLA activities, including large and small purchases, and GSA schedule purchases. Responsible for managing the life cycle contracting process in support of the DLA mission, and providing the highest quality contracting and customer service. DLA field activities may purchase similar items at the small purchase level and, under competitive circumstances, up to a threshold of $250,000.

In addition, provides general contracting in support of the DLA HQ COMPLEX, Fort Belvoir, VA and other DASC supported customers. All contracting on a Fee-For-Service basis.

Defense National Stockpile Center
8725 John J. Kingman Road
Suite 4616
Fort Belvoir, VA 22060-6223
(703) 767-5505

Principal interests: Manages the nation's reserves of strategic and critical materials for times of national emergency. Procures and sells aluminum, beryllium, cobalt, germanium, lead, manganese, mercury, mica, and rubber.

Television-Audio Support Activity
3116 Peacekeeper Way
McClellan AFB, CA 95652-1068
(916) 364-4223

Principal interests: A wide variety of Radio and Television Broadcast Equipment for all DoD activities worldwide. Procures video camcorders (all formats), broadcast TV equipment, recorders/reproducers, transmitters, switchers, monitors, cameras, color laser copiers, graphics systems, and test equipment that is used to support the Broadcast and Audio/Video Equipment.

PRODUCTS AND SERVICES BOUGHT BY
THE ARMY AND DEFENSE LOGISTICS AGENCY
MILITARY PURCHASING OFFICES*

Supplies and Equipment

10	WEAPONS
1005-35	Guns, A-1, A-6, D-1
1040	Chemical Weapons, A-6, D-3
1045-55	Launchers, A-3, D-3
1075	Degaussing and Mine Sweeping, D-3
1080	Camouflage and Deception Equipment, A-3, D-3
11	NUCLEAR ORDNANCE - A-6, A-7
12	FIRE CONTROL EQUIPMENT - A-6, A-3, A-8, D-1
13	AMMUNITION AND EXPLOSIVES
1305-20	Ammunition, A-1, A-2
1325	Bombs, A-1
1330	Grenades, A-1
1336	Missile Warheads, A-3, A-6
1337	Missile and Space Propulsion, A-3
1340	Rockets, A-1, A-3, A-6
1345	Land Mines, A-1
1370	Pyrotechnics, A-1
1375	Demolition Materials, A-1
1376	Bulk Explosives, A-1
1390	Fuzes and Primers, A-1, A-7

*Products and Services Bought by the Department of Navy Major Purchasing Offices can be found on the World Wide Web at: http://www.abm.rda.hq.navy.mil, click on "Business Opportunities" and stroll down to DoN Marketing Opportunities.

Products and Services Bought by the Department of Air Force Major Purchasing Offices can also be found on the World Wide Web at: http://selltoairforce.org. Additional information on DoD wide acquisitions by four digit federal supply code may be founded at website: http://www.acq.osd.mil/sadbu.
.

14	GUIDED MISSILES
1410-27	Guided Missile Systems and Components, A-3
1430	Remote Control Systems, A-3, D-1
1440	Launchers, A-3, D-1
1450	Handling and Servicing Equipment, A-3, D-1
15	AIRCRAFT
1510	Fixed Wing, A-3
1520	Rotary Wing, A-3, A-5
1550	Drones, A-3
1560	Airframe Components, A-3, D-3
16	AIRCRAFT COMPONENTS AND ACCESSORIES
1610	Propellers, A-3
1615	Helicopter Rotors, A-3, D-1
1620	Landing Gear Components, A-3
1650	Hydraulic Vacuum De-icing, A-3, D-1
1660	Air Conditioning and Heating Equipment, A-3, D-1
1670	Parachutes, Recovery and Tie-down, A-3, D-3
1680	Miscellaneous Accessories and Components, A-3, D-3
17	AIRCRAFT LAUNCHING, LANDING, AND GROUND HANDLING EQUIPMENT
1710	Arresting Equipment, D-1
1720	Launching Equipment, D-1
1730	Ground Servicing Equipment, A-3, D-1
1740	Specialized Trucks and Trailers, A-6, D-1

18	SPACE VEHICLES - D-3
19	SHIPS, SMALL CRAFT, PONTOONS, AND FLOATING DOCKS
1920	Fishing Vessels, A-6
1935	Special Purpose Barges and Lighters, A-11, A-12
20	SHIP AND MARINE EQUIPMENT - A-3, D-3
22	RAILWAY EQUIPMENT - A-3, A-20
23	MOTOR VEHICLES, TRAILERS, CYCLES - A-6, A-9, A-12
24	TRACTORS - D-4
25	VEHICULAR EQUIPMENT COMPONENTS - A-11, D-1
26	TIRES AND TUBES
2610	Pneumatic, Except Aircraft, A-6
2620	Pneumatic, Aircraft, D-1
2640	Tire Rebuilding - Repair Material, A-6, A-11
28	ENGINES, TURBINES, AND COMPONENTS
2805	Reciprocating Engines, Except Aircraft, A-3, D-1
2810	Reciprocating Engines, Aircraft and Components, D-5
2815	Diesel Engines and Components, A-6, A-3, A-11, D-1
2825	Steam Turbines and Components, D-1
2835	Gas Turbines and Jet Engines, Except Aircraft, A-4, D-3
2840	Gas Turbines and Jet Engines, Aircraft, A-3, D-3
2845	Rocket Engines and Components, A-3, D-4
2895	Miscellaneous Engines and Components, A-6, D-1
29	ENGINE ACCESSORIES
	For Aircraft Engines, A-3, D-3 Other Than for Aircraft Engines, A-3, A-6, D-1
30	MECHANICAL POWER TRANSMISSION EQUIPMENT - A-3, A-6, D-1
31	BEARINGS - A-3, A-6, D-4
32	WOODWORKING MACHINERY AND EQUIPMENT - Local Purchase
34	METALWORKING MACHINERY - A-1, D-3, and Local Purchase
35	SERVICE AND TRADE EQUIPMENT - D-3, and Local Purchase
36	SPECIAL INDUSTRY MACHINERY - A-1, D-3, and Local Purchase
37	AGRICULTURAL MACHINERY AND EQUIPMENT - D-4 and Local Purchase

38	CONSTRUCTION, MINING, EXCAVATING, AND HIGHWAY MAINTENANCE EQUIPMENT A-12, D-1, and Local Purchase
39	MATERIALS HANDLING EQUIPMENT - A-6, A-11, D-4, and Local Purchase
40	ROPE, CABLE, CHAIN, AND FITTINGS - D-4
41	REFRIGERATION AND AIR CONDITIONING EQUIPMENT - A-3, D-3, and Local Purchase
42	FIRE FIGHTING, RESCUE, AND SAFETY EQUIPMENT
4210	Fire Fighting Equipment, A-3, D-1
4220	Marine Lifesaving and Diving Equipment, D-1
4230	Decontaminating and Impregnating Equipment, A-1, D-3
4240	Safety and Rescue Equipment, A-3, A-6, D-3
43	PUMPS AND COMPRESSORS - A-3, A-6, D-1
44	FURNACE, STEAM PLANT, DRYING EQUIPMENT, AND NUCLEAR REACTORS
4430	Industrial Furnaces, Kilns, Lehrs, and Ovens, D-4
44XX	All Other, D-1
45	PLUMBING, HEATING, AND SANITATION EQUIPMENT - A-3, D-4
46	WATER PURIFICATION AND SEWAGE TREATMENT EQUIPMENT - A-3, D-1, D-4
47	PIPE, TUBING, HOSE, AND FITTINGS - A-1, A-3, A-12, D-1
48	VALVES - A-3, A-12, D-1
49	MAINTENANCE AND REPAIR SHOP EQUIPMENT
4910	Motor Vehicle Maintenance Equipment, A-1, A-11, D-4
4920	Aircraft Maintenance Equipment, A-4, D-3
4921	Torpedo Maintenance Equipment, D-3
4927	Rocket Maintenance Equipment, A-3, D-3
4930	Lubrication and Fuel Dispensing Equipment, A-3, D-1
4931	Fire Control Maintenance Equipment, A-1, A-3, D-1
4935	Guided Missile Maintenance Equipment, A-3, D-1
4940	Miscellaneous Maintenance Equipment, A-1, A-4, D-1, D-4
51	HAND TOOLS - D-3
52	MEASURING TOOLS - D-3 and Local Purchase
53	HARDWARE AND ABRASIVES - A-3, D-3, D-4

54	PREFABRICATED STRUCTURES AND SCAFFOLDING - A-3, A-12, D-1, and Local Purchase
55	LUMBER, MILLWORK, PLYWOOD, AND VENEER - A-12, D-4, and Local Purchase
56	CONSTRUCTION AND BUILDING MATERIALS - A-12, D-4 and Local Purchase
58	COMMUNICATION EQUIPMENT - A-3, A-4, A-5, A-8, A-11, A-12, D-1, D-6 and Local Purchase
59	ELECTRICAL AND ELECTRONIC EQUIPMENT COMPONENTS - A-1, A-3, A-4, A-5, A-6, D-1, D-4
60	FIBER OPTICS - A-3, A-4, D-1
61	ELECTRIC WIRE AND POWER DISTRIBUTION EQUIPMENT
6105	Electrical Motors, A-3, A-4, D-3
6110	Electrical Control Equipment, A-1, A-4, A-12, D-3
6115	Generators and Generator Sets, A-3, A-4, A-12, D-3
6120	Transformers, D-3
6125	Converters, Rotating, D-3
6130	Converters, Nonrotating, A-3, D-3
6135	Primary Batteries, A-3, A-4, D-3
6140	Secondary Batteries, A-4, D-3
6145	Wire and Cable, Electrical, D-3
6150	Miscellaneous Electrical Equipment, A-4, A-12, D-3
62	LIGHTING FIXTURES AND LAMPS
6210	Outdoor Lighting, D-3
6220	Vehicle Lights, A-3, D-3
62XX	All Other, D-3
63	ALARM AND SIGNAL SYSTEMS
6320	Shipboard, D-3
6340	Aircraft, A-3, D-3
6350	Miscellaneous, A-3, D-3
65	MEDICAL, DENTAL, AND VETERINARY EQUIPMENT - A-9, A-10, D-5
66	INSTRUMENTS AND LABORATORY EQUIPMENT
6605	Navigational Instruments, A-3, A-4, D-3
6610	Flight Instruments, A-3, D-3

6615	Autopilots, Airborne Gyro, A-4, D-3
6620	Engine Instruments, A-3, A-5, D-3
6625	Electrical and Electronic Measuring Instruments, A-2, A-3, A-4, A-6, A-11, D-1
6630	Chemical Analysis Instruments, A-2, A-5, D-5
6635	Physical Properties Testing Equipment, A-2, A-5, D-3
6636	Environmental Chambers, A-2, A-5, D-3
6640	Laboratory Equipment and Supplies, A-2, A-4, A-5, A-9, D-5
6645	Time Measuring Instruments, A-5, D-3
6650	Optical Instruments, A-1, A-2, A-5, A-6, D-3
6660	Meteorological Instruments, A-4, D-3
6665	Hazard-Detecting Instruments, A-1, A-2, A-4, A-5, A-4, D-3
6670	Scales and Balances, A-5, D-3
6675	Drafting, Surveying, and Mapping Instruments, A-3, D-3
6680	Motion-Measuring Instruments, A-3, A-5, D-3
6685	Pressure, Temperature, and Humidity Instruments, A-2, A-3, A-5, D-3
6695	Combination and Miscellaneous Instruments, A-2, A-3, A-5, D-3
67	PHOTOGRAPHIC EQUIPMENT - D-3
68	CHEMICALS AND CHEMICAL PRODUCTS - A-2, A-5, A-6, A-12, D-3, D-5
69	TRAINING AIDS AND DEVICES - A-3, A-8, D-3
70	GENERAL PURPOSE ADPE AND SUPPORT
70XX	Local Purchase for All Codes
7010	ADPE Configuration, A-4, A-5
7025	Input/Output and Storage Devices, A-3, A-4, A-5, A-7, A-14, D-1, D-6
7030	ADP Software, A-3, A-4, A-5, A-7, A-8, D-6
7035	ADP Support Equipment, A-3, A-4, A-5, A-7, A-11, D-6
7042	Mini- and Micro-Computer Controls, D-6
7045	ADP Supplies and Support Equipment, A-3, A-4, A-5, A-7, A-12, D-6
7050	ADP Components, A-3, A-4, A-5, A-12, D-6
71	FURNITURE
71XX	Local Purchase for All Codes
7105	Household Furniture, D-3

7110	Office Furniture, A-7, D-3
7125	Cabinets, Lockers, Bins, and Shelving, D-3
72	HOUSEHOLD AND COMMERCIAL FURNISHINGS AND APPLIANCES - D-3, D-5 and Local Purchase
73	FOOD PREPARATION AND SERVING EQUIPMENT
7310	Food Cooking, Baking, and Serving Equipment, D-4
7320	Kitchen Equipment and Appliances, D-4
7330	Kitchen Hand Tools and Utensils, D-4
7340	Cutlery and Flatware, D-4
7350	Tableware, D-4
7360	Food Preparation and Serving Kits and Outfits, A-3, D-4
74	OFFICE MACHINES AND VISIBLE RECORD EQUIPMENT - D-3, Local Purchase
75	OFFICE SUPPLIES AND DEVICES - D-3, Local Purchase
76	BOOKS, MAPS, AND OTHER PUBLICATIONS - D-3, Local Purchase
77	MUSICAL INSTRUMENTS, PHONOGRAPHS, AND HOMETYPE RADIOS - Local Purchase
78	RECREATIONAL AND ATHLETIC EQUIPMENT - Local Purchase
79	CLEANING EQUIPMENT AND SUPPLIES - D-3
80	BRUSHES, PAINTS, SEALERS, AND ADHESIVES - Local Purchase
81	CONTAINERS, PACKAGING, AND PACKING SUPPLIES
8105	Bags and Sacks, D-3
8110	Drums and Cans, D-4
8115	Boxes and Cartons, Local Purchase
8120	Gas Cylinders, D-3
8125	Bottles and Jars, D-4
8130	Reels and Spools, D-4 and Local Purchase
8135	Packaging and Packing Materials, D-3, D-4 and Local Purchase
8140	Ordnance Boxes, A-1, A-8, D-3
8145	Specialized Shipping and Storage Containers, A-3, D-3
83	TEXTILES, LEATHER, FURS, APPAREL, AND SHOE FINDINGS, TENTS, AND FLAGS - D-5
84	CLOTHING, INDIVIDUAL EQUIPMENT, AND INSIGNIA

8475	Specialized Flight Clothing and Accessories, D-5
84XX	All Other Clothing Codes, D-5
85	TOILETRIES - D-3
87	AGRICULTURAL SUPPLIES
8710	Forage and Feed
8720-30	Fertilizer, Seeds, and Nursery Stock, Local Purchase
89	SUBSISTENCE
8905	Meat, Poultry, and Fish, D-5, and Local Purchase
8910	Dairy Foods and Eggs, D-5, and Local Purchase
8915	Fruits and Vegetables, D-5, and Local Purchase
8920	Bakery and Cereal Products, D-6, D-7, and Local Purchase
8925	Sugar, Confectionery, and Nuts, D-5
8930	Jams and Jellies, D-5
8935	Soups and Bouillon, D-6
8940	Special Dietary Foods, D-5
8945	Food Oils and Fats, D-5
8950	Condiments, D-5
8955	Coffee, Tea, and Cocoa, D-5, and Local Purchase
8960	Beverages, Nonalcoholic, D-5, and Local Purchase
8970	Composite Food Packages, D-5
8975	Tobacco Products, D-5 and Local Purchase
91	FUELS, LUBRICANTS, OILS, AND WAXES
9110	Solid Fuels, D-2
9130	Petroleum Base Liquid Propellants and Fuel, D-2 and Local Purchase
9140	Fuel Oils, D-2, and Local Purchase
9150	Oils, Greases - Cutting, Lubricating, and Hydraulic, D-2
9160	Miscellaneous Waxes, Oils, and Fats, D-4
93	NONMETALLIC FABRICATED MATERIALS - D-3, and Local Purchase
95	METAL BARS, SHEETS, AND SHAPES
9505	Wire, Nonelectrical, Iron and Steel, D-4
9510	Bars and Rods, Iron and Steel, D-4
9515	Sheet and Strip, Iron and Steel, D-4

9520   Structural Shapes, Iron and Steel, A-12, D-4

9525   Wire, Nonelectrical, Nonferrous, D-4

9530   Bars and Rods, Nonferrous, D-4

9535   Sheet and Strip, Nonferrous, D-5 and Local Purchase

9540   Structural Shapes, Nonferrous, D-4

96   ORES, MINERALS, AND THEIR PRIMARY PRODUCTS, D-4

Services

H1   QUALITY CONTROL SERVICE

J   MAINTENANCE, REPAIR, AND REBUILDING OF EQUIPMENT

J013   Ammunition and Explosives, A-1

J014   Guided Missiles, A-3

J015   Aircraft, A-3, and Local Purchase

J016   Aircraft Components, A-3, and Local Purchase

J017   Aircraft Ground Equipment, Local Purchase

J020   Marine Equipment, A-3, A-12

J023   Vehicles, Trailers, and Cycles, Local Purchase

J028   Engines and Turbines, A-3

J034   Metalwork Machinery, A-1, D-3

J036   Industrial Machinery, A-1, Local Purchase

J041   Refrigeration and Air Conditioning, A-3, Local Purchase

J042   Fire Rescue and Safety Equipment, A-3

J058   Communication Equipment, A-4, A-5, and Local Purchase

J065   Medical and Dental Equipment, A-10

J066   Instruments and Lab Equipment, A-5, and Local Purchase

J070   ADP Equipment and Supplies, Local Purchase

J074   Office Machines, Local Purchase

K   MODIFICATION OF EQUIPMENT

K010   Weapons, A-1

K012   Fire Control Equipment, A-3

K013   Ammunition and Explosives, A-1, A-2

K014   Guided Missiles, A-3

K015 Aircraft, A-3

K016 Aircraft Components, A-3

K017 Aircraft Ground Equipment, A-3

K058 Communication Equipment, A-4, A-5

L   TECHNICAL REPRESENTATIVE SERVICES

M   OPERATION OF GOVERNMENT-OWNED FACILITY

[There are more opportunities than you might have thought, including operation of buildings, utilities, and other facilities. Observe the Government operations in your area and consider whether they may be contractor-operated. Government policy is to encourage contractor operation where it is in the Government's interest.]

N   INSTALLATION OF EQUIPMENT

N058 Communication Equipment, A-4, A-5

N068 Chemical Products, A-2, A-5

P   SALVAGE SERVICES (Including demolition) - A-12 and Local Purchase

Q   MEDICAL SERVICES [Note: Specialized services and specialized suppliers], A-10

R   PROFESSIONAL TECHNICAL AND MANAGEMENT SERVICES

R2XX Architect-Engineer

R301 ADP Facility Management, A-7

R302 ADP Systems Development and Programming, A-5, A-6, A-7, A-12, and Local Purchase

R303 ADP Entry, A-7

R407 Program Evaluation, A-2, A-4

R408 Program Management-Support, A-2, A-3, A-4, A-7

R412 Simulations A-2, A-3

R414 Systems Engineering, A-4, A-3, A-6, and Local Purchase

R415 Technology Sharing, A-2

R425 Engineering Technical Services, Local Purchase , A-2, A-4

R504 Studies/Chemical-Biological, A-2

R551 mobilization/Preparedness Studies, A-2

R702 Data Collection Services, A-6

R706 Logistics Support Services, A-2, A-4

R707	Procurement and Acquisition Support Services, A-3
S	UTILITIES AND HOUSEKEEPING SERVICES
S201	Custodial-Janitorial, Local Purchase
S203	Food Service, Local Purchase
S205	Garbage Collection, Local Purchase
S206	Guard Services, Local Purchase
S208	Landscaping and Ground keeping, Local Purchase
T	PHOTOGRAPHIC, MAPPING, PRINTING, AND PUBLICATION
T013	TECHNICAL WRITING, A-3, A-4
V	TRANSPORTATION AND TRAVEL [Note: Specialized services and specialized suppliers, A-8
W	LEASE OR RENTAL OF EQUIPMENT
W038	Rental of Construction Equipment, A-12
W070	Rental of ADP Equipment, Local Purchase
W074	Rental of Office Machines, Local Purchase
X	LEASE OR RENTAL OF FACILITIES
X173	Rental of Fuel Storage Buildings, D-3
Y	CONSTRUCTION - A-3, A-12
Z	MAINTENANCE AND REPAIR OF REAL ESTATE - A-21, and Local Purchase

---

Note: If you have special capability in connection with particular items or lines of equipment, you should let the producer of that equipment be aware of your interest in working with it. You may be able to get subcontract work or to learn of DoD locations that have the equipment.

Chapter 3:

RESEARCH AND DEVELOPMENT SALES OPPORTUNITIES

MAJOR MILITARY RESEARCH AND DEVELOPMENT ACTIVITIES

The DoD encourages participation by small concerns, including those owned by women and by disadvantaged persons, in its R&D programs. DoD seeks the most advanced scientific knowledge attainable and the best possible equipment and systems that can be devised and produced. It is the government's policy (FAR 35.008), in awarding an R&D contract, to select the organization ". . . that proposes the best ideas or concepts and has the highest competence in the specific field of science or technology involved." You should evaluate your firm critically before seeking a government R&D contract. Be sure that your firm is as well qualified as others who may want the same award. The telephone numbers in the lists which follow are for the small business specialists at the research organizations. Also, refer to Part 1 of this book, for information on the DoD Small Business Innovation Research (SBIR) program.

DEPARTMENT OF THE ARMY

U. S. Army Space & Missile Defense Command (205) 955-3412
PO Box 1500
Huntsville, AL 35807-3801

Principal interests: Manages technology base research and development for Ballistic Missile Defense Organization and provides significant technical and program support to the Army Program Executive Office for Air and Missile Defense; supports Army space requirements; develops and demonstrates technologies required for kinetic energy weapons, directed energy weapons, structures, materials; conducts lethality and vulnerability analysis of various threat objects; conducts research in the areas of optics, radar and laser radar technology, high-performance electronics, sensor phenomenology, analysis, and measurement programs; develops theater and strategic missile targets for all of DoD; pursues innovative, high-risk, high-payoff research programs in acoustic-optical processing, laser satellite communications, radar range-doppler images, and threat destruction mechanisms.

U. S. Army Research Office (919) 549-4271
AMXRO-PR
PO 12211
Research Triangle Park, NC 27709-2211

Principal interests: Research proposals on a competitive basis, from educational institutions, nonprofit organizations, and private industry in the fields of mathematics, physics, engineering, chemistry, electronics, materials, biology and geoscience.

U. S. Army Research Laboratory (301) 394-3692
AMSCL-SB
2800 Powder Mill Road
Adelphia, MD 20783-1197

Principal interests: Research and technology development efforts provide scientific and technological innovation in ten fields of technical endeavor; lethality; survivability enhancement, assessment; sensors, signatures and signal processing, power resources; materials and structures; battlefield environmental effects; human factors; advanced computing and advanced electronics.

U. S. Army Aviation and Missile Command (205) 876-5441
ATTN: AMSAM-SB
Redstone Arsenal
Huntsville, AL 35898-5150

Principal Interests: R&D of new helicopter systems, support of qualification testing of turbine engines, development and evaluation of prototype hardware for fueling and defueling equipment for use in combat areas and solving fuel contamination problems. Conducts research in both exploratory and advanced development in subsonic areas of application. R&D associated with free rockets, guided missiles, ballistic missiles, targets, air defense weapons systems, fire control coordination equipment, related special purpose and multisystem test equipment, missile launching and ground support equipment, metrology and calibration equipment, and other associated equipment.

Associated Installations:

Propulsion Directorate (216) 433-3703
NASA/Lewis Research Center
2100 Brookpart Road
Cleveland, OH 44135-3127

Aerostructures Directorate (804) 864-2447
NASA/Langley Research Center
Hampton, VA 23665-5225

U. S. Army Soldiers Systems Command (508) 233-4995
ATTN: AMSS-C-SB
Kansas Street
Natick, MA 01760-5008

Principal interests: R&D in the physical and biological sciences and engineering to meet military requirements in commodity areas of textiles, clothing, body armor, footwear, insecticides and fungicides, subsistence, containers, food service, equipment (as assigned) tentage and equipage, and air delivery equipment.

U. S. Army Communications-Electronics Command (908) 532-4511
ATTN: AMSEL-SB
Fort Monmouth, NJ 07703-5005

Principal interests: R&D and acquisition, to include first production and initial fielding of communications, tactical data, and command and control systems. R&D programs related to communications, electronics intelligence, electronic warfare, reconnaissance surveillance, target acquisition, night vision, combat identification, position locations, tactical satellites, maneuver control, common hardware/software, sensors, power sources and other associated equipment.

U. S. Army Tank Automotive & Armaments Command (810) 574-5388
ATTN: AMSTA-CB
Warren, MI 48397-5000

Principal interests: R&D associated with combat tactical and special purpose vehicles. R&D programs related to advanced concepts, development and engineering of combat and tactical vehicles, including automotive subsystems and components. Component programs involved engines, transmissions, suspensions, electrical and miscellaneous vehicular components.

U. S. Army Armament Research, (201) 724-4106
Development and Engineering Center
AMSTA-AR-SB
Picatinny Arsenal, NJ 07806-5000

Principal interests: Product development/improvement of munitions, weaponry, and fire control systems; testing and analysis; and technical support for fielded armament systems.

U. S. Army Test & Evaluation Command (410) 278-1201
ATTN AMSTE-PR
Aberdeen Proving Ground, MD 21005-5005

Associated installations:

U. S. Army Garrison (410) 278-1548
ATTN: STEAP-SB
Aberdeen Proving Ground, MD 21005-5001

Principal Interests: R&D, production and post production testing of weapons, systems, ammunition, combat and support vehicles, and individual equipment.

U. S. Army Dugway Proving Ground (801) 831-2102
ATTN: STEDP-DBO-DOC
Dugway, UT 84022-5202

Principal interests: Conducts field and laboratory tests to evaluate chemical and radiological weapons and defense systems and materiel, as well as defense research.

U. S. Army White Sands Missile Range (505) 678-1401
ATTN: STEWS-SBA
White Sands, NM 88002-5031

Principal interests: Conducts testing and evaluation of Army missiles and rockets. Operates the United States only land based national range to support missile and other testing for the Army, Air Force, Navy, and National Aeronautics and Space Administration.

U. S. Army Yuma Proving Ground (602) 328-6285
ATTN: STEYP-CR
Yuma Proving Ground, AZ 85365-9102

Principal interests: R&D, production and post production testing of weapons, systems, ammunition, and combat and support vehicles. Conducts environmental tests, air drop and air delivery tests, and participates in engineering testing of combat end support items

U. S. Army Engineer Waterways Experiment Station (601) 634-2424
3909 Halls Ferry Road
Vicksburg, MS 39180-6199

Principal interests: Research in support of the civil and military mission of the Chief of Engineers and other Federal agencies, through the operation of laboratories in the broad fields of hydraulics, soil mechanics, concrete, engineering geology, rock mechanics, pavements, expedient construction, nuclear and conventional weapons, protective structures, vehicle mobility, environmental relationships, aquatic weeds, water quality, dredge material and nuclear and chemical explosives excavation.

U. S. Army Cold Regions Research and (603) 646-4324
Engineering Laboratory
72 Lyme Road
Hanover, NH 03755-1290

Principal interests: Research pertaining to characteristics and events unique to cold regions, especially winter conditions, including design of facilities, structures, and equipment and methods for building, traveling, living, and working in cold environments.

U. S. Army Construction-Engineering Research (217) 373-6748
Laboratory
2902 Newmark Drive
Campaign, IL 61826-1305

Principal interests: Research in the materials, utilities, energy, and structures of all buildings except those specifically designed for cold regions. Conducts systems oriented R&D on the life-cycle requirements of military facilities and their management (the life cycle includes all the processes of planning, design, and construction through maintenance and disposition). Integrates technological developments into construction. Develops corrosion mitigation systems for structures utilizing improved organic coatings, cathodic protection methods, and alternative materials selection. Develops procedures and technology to protect and enhance environmental quality.

U. S. Army Topographic Engineering Center (703) 428-6608
7701 Telegraph Road, Building 2592
Fort Belvoir, Virginia 22301-3864
Web Site: http://www.tec.army.mil

Principal interests: R&D in the topographic sciences including mapping, charting, geodesy, space research, remote sensing, spectral characterization and analysis, point positioning, surveying and land navigation, environmental support, computer image generation and 3-D battlefield visualizations, modeling and simulation, and distributed interactive simulations. Provides scientific and technical advisory services to support geographic intelligence and environmental resources requirements.

U. S. Army Medical Research & Materiel Command (301) 619-2471
U. S. Army Medical Research Acquisition Activity
MCMR-AAU
820 Chandler Street
Ft. Detrick, MD 21702-1014

Principal interests: Basic and applied medical research and product development. Medical laboratory and logistical support services, supplies, equipment, and telecommunications.

Associated Activities:

U. S. Army Aeromedical Research Laboratory
(334) 255-6908
MCMR-UAC-E
Fort Rucker, AL 36362-5292

U. S. Army Institute of Surgical Research
(210) 916-2250
MCMR-USX
3400 Rayley E. Chambers Avenue
Fort Sam Houston, TX 78234-6315

U. S. Army Medical Materiel Development Activity
(301) 619-7584
MCMR-UMS-R
622 Neiman Street
Fort Detrick, MD 21702-5009

U. S. Army Medical Research Institute of Chemical Defense
(410) 671-1834
MCMR-UV-RC
Aberdeen Proving Ground, MD 21010-5425

U. S. Army Research Institute of Environmental Medicine
(508) 651-4817
MCMR-UE-RP
Natick, MA 01760-5007

U. S. Army Medical Research Institute of Infectious Diseases
MCMR-UIZ-M
1425 Porter Street
Fort Detrick, MD 21702-5011

Walter Reed Army Institute of Research
(202) 782-3061
MCMR-UWZ-C
Bldg 40, Walter Reed Army Medical Center
Washington, D. C. 20307-5100

Telemedicine Research Laboratory
(301) 619-7917
MCMR-AT
504 Scott Street
Fort Detrick, MD 21702-5012

DEPARTMENT OF THE NAVY

Office of Naval Research
(703) 696-8528
ONR 362 SBIR
800 North Quincy Street, Room 502
Arlington, VA 22217-5000

Principal interests: Basic research and technology. Contracts are generally awarded in response to unsolicited proposals. The major areas of interest are: mathematical and physical sciences; environmental sciences; engineering sciences; life sciences; aviation and aerospace technology; undersea technology; integrated antisubmarine warfare; surface warfare and supporting technologies; manpower, personnel, and training technology; and advanced conformal submarine acoustic sensor.

Navy Personnel Research and Development Center
(619) 553-7805
Code 022
San Diego, CA 92152-6800

Principal interests: Research in manpower, personnel, education and training, and human factors engineering in development and operation of Navy personnel systems.

National Naval Medical Center
(301) 295-0285
Procurement Department
8901 Wisconsin Avenue, Bldg. 54
Bethesda, MD 20889-5000

Principal interests: Research, development, test, and evaluation in the following technology areas: submarine medicine, aviation medicine, electromagnetic radiation, human performance, fleet health care, infectious diseases, oral and dental health.

Naval Air Systems Command
(703) 692-0935
Code 02E, Room 424
1421 Jefferson Davis Highway
Arlington, VA 22243-2000

Principal interests: Design, development, testing, and evaluation of airframes, aircraft engines, components, and fuels and lubricants; airborne electronic equipment, pyrotechnics, and mine countermeasures equipment; air launched weapons systems and underwater sound systems; aircraft drone and target systems; catapults, arresting gear, visual landing aids, meteorological equipment, ground handling equipment, parachutes, flight clothing, and survival equipment.

Space and Naval Warfare Systems Command
(619)524-7701
Code SPA-OOK
4301 Pacific Highway
San Diego, CA 92110-3127

Principal interests: RDT&E for command, control and communications; undersea and space surveillance; electronic warfare; navigational aids; electronic test equipment; electronic materials, components and devices.

Naval Facilities Engineering Command
(703) 325-8549
Code FAC-OOJ
200 Stovall Street, Room 11N59
Alexandria, VA 22332-5000

Principal interests: R&D for new or improved materials, equipment, or engineering techniques to resolve specific engineering problems pertaining to design, construction, operation, and maintenance of shore facilities.

Naval Sea Systems Command

(703) 602-1964
Code SEA-02K
2531 Jefferson Davis Highway
Arlington, VA 22242-5160

Principal interests: R&D, procurement, and logistics support and other material functions for all ships and craft, shipboard weapon systems and ordnance, air launched mines and torpedoes, shipboard components such as propulsion sonar search radar and auxiliary equipment; procurement, technical guidance, and supervision of operations related to salvage of stranded or sunk ships and craft.

Naval Supply Systems Command
(717)790-3575
Building 9
P.O. Box 2050
Mechanicsburg, PA 17055-0791

Principal interests: R&D in supply systems management techniques, including mathematical and statistical analyses, materials handling, clothing and textiles, transportation, and logistics data processing systems.

Naval Research Laboratory
(202) 767-6263
Contracts Division, Code 3204, Bldg. 57
4555 Overlook Avenue, SW
Washington, DC 20375-5326

Principal interests: Scientific research and advanced technology development for new and improved materials, equipment, techniques, systems and related operational procedures for the Navy. Fields of interest include space science and systems; environmental sciences; plasma physics; acoustics; radar; electronic warfare; marine technology; chemistry; materials; optical and radiation sciences; electronics and information technology.

Naval Construction Battalion Center
(805) 982-5066
Code 10G/27G, Bldg 41
1000 23rd Avenue
Port Hueneme, CA 93043-4301

Principal interests: RDT&E center for shore and seafloor facilities and for the support of Navy and Marine Corps construction forces.
Naval Underwater Warfare Center

(401) 841-2442
Code OOSB Ext. 270
1176 Howell Street, Bldg. 11
Newport, RI 02840

Principal interests: Submarine warfare analysis, combat systems engineering and integration, acoustic reconnaissance and search systems, electronic warfare systems, command and control systems, combat control systems, submarine unique communications systems, submarine launchers, submarine-launched torpedoes, submarine unique antisubmarine warfare tactical missile systems, underwater acoustics for system performance prediction, subsurface target simulators, and undersea range development and operation.

Naval Air Warfare Center
(301) 342-7567
Aircraft Division, Code 20C00W Ext. 103
Contracts Building 588, Suite 2
22347 Cedar Point Road, Unit 6
Patuxent River, MD 20670-1161

Principal interests: RDT&E of aircraft weapons systems, command and control systems, subsystems and components, external stores ordnance and explosive devices for aircraft, electrical and electronics both air and ship systems, instrumentation, data management and analyses, reliability and maintainability (R&M), integrated logistics support (ILS), systems
safety, simulation planning and analysis, flight services and program operation, flight services and program operation, program training management, computer programming and operations, software/hardware integration and analysis, electronic, computer, and communication laboratory operational support, software/hardware risk management.

Naval Air Warfare Center
(760) 939-2712
Weapons Division, Code 00K000D
One Administration Circle
China Lake, CA 93555-6001

Principal interests: RDT&E center for air warfare systems (except antisubmarine warfare systems) and missile weapons systems including missile propulsion, warheads, fuses, avionics and fire control, missile guidance, and the national range/facility for parachute test and evaluation.

Naval Air Warfare Center
(407) 380-8253
Training Systems Division
Code 86D1/27B
12350 Research Parkway
Orlando, FL 32826-3224

Principal interests: Research investigations and exploratory development in simulation technology and techniques, investigations and studies in the fields of training psychology, human factors and human engineering, design and engineering development of training devices, weapons system trainers and simulators, and technical data and related ancillary support materials and services.

Naval Surface Warfare Center
(301) 227-2871
Carderock Division
Building 30, Code 303
9500 McArthur Blvd, Room 1
West Bethesda, MD 20817-5700

Principal interests: New vehicle concepts, ship and aircraft compatibility, ship trials and the development of vehicle technology. Areas addressed include hull form; structures; systems development and analysis; Marine Corps systems; fleet support; survivability, vulnerability, protection and weapons effects; propulsion; silencing; maneuvering and control auxiliary machinery; structural, propulsion and machinery materials; environmental effects, pollution abatement, alternate energy sources (non nuclear); logistics research and information systems; engineering development and design of specialized testing equipment; computer techniques and software for analysis, design and manufacturing, and numerical mechanics. Provides RDT&E support to the U.S. Maritime Administration and the maritime industry.

Naval Air Warfare Center
(609) 538-6640
Aircraft Division
P.O. Box 7176, Code SUA
1440 Parkway Avenue
Trenton, NJ 08628-0176

Principal interests: RDT&E of aircraft propulsion systems and components and accessories and fuels and lubricants.

Naval Surface Warfare Center
(812) 854-1542
Crane Division
Code SB
300 Highway 121, Building 221A
Crane, IN 47522-5001

Principal interests: Design, engineering, evaluation, and analysis programs required in providing support for ships and crafts, shipboard weapons systems, and expendable and non expendable ordnance items.

Naval Surface Warfare Center
(301) 743-6604
Indian Head Division
Code SB
101 Strauss Avenue
Indian Head, MD 20640-5035

Principal interests: Research, development, pilot manufacture, test, and evaluation and fleet support of gun propellants, cartridges, cartridge actuated devices, and weapon system simulators. Provides process development, pilot manufacture and engineering in the transition of rocket engines and warheads from development to production. Provides design support, in-service engineering and acquisition engineering support for Navy rocket engines.

Naval Weapons Station
(804) 887-4644
Supply Department, Code 113
P.O. Box 140
Yorktown, VA 23691-0140

Principal interests: Development of weapons and explosive loading equipment.

Naval Oceanographic Office
(601) 689-8369
Contracts Office, Code N4212, Bldg. 9134
Stennis Space Center, MS 39522-5001

Principal interests: R&D in oceanographic, hydrographic, and geodetic equipment, techniques, and systems.

Naval Surface Warfare Center
(703) 663-4806
Dahlgren Division, Code C6
Dahlgren, VA 22448-5000

Principal interests: Provide RDT&E, engineering and fleet support for surface warfare systems, surface ship combat systems, ordnance, mines, amphibious warfare systems, mine countermeasures special warfare systems, and strategic systems.

Naval Surface Warfare Center
(904) 234-4347
Dahlgren Division
Coastal Systems Station, Code 20D
6703 West Highway 98
Panama City, FL 32407-5000

Principal interests: Provide RDT&E for mines and countermeasures, special warfare, amphibious warfare, diving and other naval missions that take place primarily in the coastal region.

Naval Air Warfare Center (805) 989-8914
Weapons Division, Code P65
Point Mugu, CA 93041-5000

Principal interests: Performs test and evaluation, development and follow-on engineering; provides logistics and training support for naval weapons, weapon systems, and related devices; and provides major range, technical, and base support for fleet users and other DoD and government agencies. Functions relate to guided missiles, rockets, free-fall weapons, fire control and radar systems, drones and target drones, computers, electronic warfare devices and countermeasures equipment, range services and instrumentation, test planning simulations, and data collection.

Space and Navy Warfare System Center
(619) 553-4326
RDT&E Division, Code 02202
53570 Silvergate Avenue
San Diego, CA 92152-5113

Principal interests: RDT&E for command control, communications, ocean surveillance, surface and air-launched undersea weapon systems, submarine arctic warfare, and supporting techniques.

DEPARTMENT OF THE AIR FORCE

Space and Missile System Center (SMC/BC)
(310) 363-2855
155 Discoverer Blvd, Ste 2017
Los Angeles AFB CA 90245-4692

Principle interests: The mission of SMC is to plan, program, and manage AFMC programs to acquire space systems, subsystems, support equipment, and related hardware and software; provide for the maintenance, construction, alteration, and security of launch, tracking, and support facilities; conduct research, exploratory development, and advanced development programs to support future space missions; provide for and conduct launch and flight test and evaluation support of major DoD programs and programs of other federal agencies; perform the functions of launch, launch control, deployment checkout prior to turnover, and sustaining engineering; perform on-orbit test and evaluation of systems, subsystems and components, discharge AF responsibilities for designated AF, DoD, and international space programs; plan, program, and acquire test facilities and other test investments required by AFMC programs at all locations (test centers ancontractor facilities); plan and provide for security on all systems and information requiring safeguards consistent with AF and DoD security directives; provide management oversight for commercial expendable Launch Vehicle Activity; conduct launch agreement negotiations with commercial space launch operators; provide system engineering management support for selected space systems, subsystems, facilities, support equipment, and related hardware and software; support other product divisions and federal agencies with technologies derived from its subordinate laboratories.

While there are no AF aircraft assigned to Los Angeles AFB, the operational contracting directorate does contract for all other work necessary for the operation and maintenance of the base.

HQ Air Force Space Command (HQ AFSPC/LGCM)
(719)554-5324
150 Vandenberg St, Ste 1105
Peterson AFB, CO 80914-4350

Principle interests: HQ AFSPC awards and administers contracts for AF Space Command services and associated supply requirements to support major operational defense systems, space launch operations and maintenance, satellite control, and satellite operations. This includes associated engineering and technical support services, as well as local purchase requirements for the following bases:

Buckley ANGB, Colorado
Falcon AFB, Colorado
FE Warren AFB, Wyoming
Malmstrom AFB, Montana

Onizuka AFB, California
Patrick AFB, Florida
Peterson AFB, Colorado
Vandenberg AFB, California

Human Systems Center/BC (AFMC)
(210)536-4348
8106 Chennault Rd, Bldg 1160
Brooks AFB, TX 78235-5318

Principle interests: The Human Systems Center has the role of integrating and maintaining people in AF systems and operations. People are the enabling factor in AF operations. Recognizing this, the center was established as the AF agent for human-centered research, development, acquisition, and specialized operational support. * (Also cover AF-wide environmental restoration and base closure efforts.)

The center prepares, maintains, protects, and enhances human capabilities and human-system performance, from the scope of the individual to the entire forces. The center works in four functional areas to meet current and future human-centered operational requirements:

Crew-system integration
Crew protection
Environmental protection
Force readiness (human resources and aerospace medicine)

The Armstrong Laboratory, Human Systems Program Office, the USAF School of Aerospace Medicine and an air base group are major units of the center.

HSC/BC also provides contract support to the AF Center for Environmental Excellence (AFCEE) which provides a full range of technical services in environmental areas, including contracting for full service remediation/remedial action, worldwide environmental services, preliminary assessment/site inspections, tank removals, environmental support, community relations, general systems engineering and integration (GSE&I), information clearing house, and Installation Restoration Program Information Management System (IRPIMS).

The Operational Contracting Division acquires supplies, equipment, services, construction, and utilities in support of Brooks AFB and tenant organizations.

Armstrong Laboratory
(210)536-4348
c/o Human Systems Center/BC
Brooks AFB, TX 78235-5320

Principle interests: Ensuring that the AF's weapon systems and the people operating them are compatible. The laboratory researches and develops technology for maintaining, protecting, and enhancing human capabilities during AF operations.

School of Aerospace Medicine (SAM) plans and conducts R&D on work dealing with applied aeromedical research including medical education and training, clinical evaluation/consultations, and special support activities.

Human Resources Directorate conducts exploratory and advanced development programs for manpower and personnel, operational and technical training, simulation, and logistics systems in four research divisions. Their goal is to assist the AF in achieving the best methods for acquiring enlisted and officer members; training and maintaining this force at peak readiness.

Occupational and Environmental Health Directorate provides professional consultation, specialized laboratory services, and operational field support to assist the AF in meeting its worldwide responsibilities in the management of occupational, radiological, and environmental health problems. It is a technical center for the AF's Installation Restoration Program and host for the AF Radiation Assessment Team.

Human Systems Program Directorate conducts advanced and full-scale development and acquisition programs in crew-system integration, personnel protection, air base support, computer based training systems, and clothing design in response to Air Force needs. This office is also responsible for aeromedical casualty, manpower, and personnel programs; advanced anti-G system for fighter aircraft, life support/survival equipment, chemical defense, hazardous waste cleanup, integrated aircrew protection, space crew enhancement technology, cockpit design, helmet mounted systems (night vision, etc.), crew escape technology, and noise (sonic boom impact) technology.

Science, Technology and Operational Aeromedical Support Program Office develops technology for future warfighting capabilities by generating the strategy to produce the enabling human centered technology options.

Drug Testing Directorate implements the AF drug abuse program, conducts testing for known drugs of abuse, such as cocaine, amphetamines, barbiturates and marijuana for CONUS AF members and Army personnel in the South Central US, as well as research and testing on other drugs to ensure drug users are deterred from switching to substances not currently being analyzed.

Phillips Laboratory (PL/BC)
(505)846-8515
2000 Wyoming Blvd SE, Bldg 2064
Kirtland AFB, NM 87117-5060

The Phillips Laboratory provides contracting support to its own activities which include the following Laboratories:

PL/GP Geophysics PL/WS Adv Weapons and Surveillance
PL/RK Propulsion PL/SX Space Experiments
PL/VT Space and Missiles Technology
PL/LI Lasers and Imaging

In addition, support is provided for acquisition of research and development projects and major support contracts to other Government agencies such as: The Air Force Operational Test and Evaluation Center (AFOTEC), Defense Advanced Research Agency(DARPA), Theater Air Command Computer Simulation Facility (TACCSF), AirBorne Laser Program Office (ABL), Space and Missile Systems Center's Space and Missile Test and Evaluation Directorate (SMC/TE), San Antonio Air Logistics Center's Nuclear Weapons Integration Facility (SA-ALC/NWI), and the U.S. Army's BIG CROW Program Office.

The Phillips Laboratory establishes and maintains comprehensive in-house resources for research, development, testing, and evaluation; manages activities of the various Phillips Laboratory centers; integrates technology products and conducts configuration research; develops and tests experimental space systems and subsystems, nonconventional and advanced weapons, and rocket propulsion systems to acquire design data and demonstrate new and integrated technology; acts as focal point or lead organization for designated programs or activities involving two or more AF or DoD organizations, or DoD and NASA organizations; acts in coordination with space test programs; advocates and sponsors space experimentation and test of assigned technologies in space.

The operational contracting division contracts for supplies, equipment, and work necessary for the operation and maintenance of Phillips Laboratory and Kirtland AFB.

Wright Laboratory
(937)255-5422
Directorate of R&D Contracting
c/o Aeronautical Systems Center (ASC/BC)
2196 D St
Wright-Patterson AFB OH 45433-7201

Principle interests: This directorate provides business and contracting support for Wright Laboratory (WL). Contracts are written for requirements of the following directorates:

Aero Propulsion and Power Directorate is responsible for development of airbreathing propulsion and aerospace power technology needed for future AF systems, as well as providing assistance to the "product divisions" of AFMC in acquiring new systems and in helping to resolve developmental and operation problems.

Avionics Directorate conducts R&D programs for aerospace reconnaissance, weapons delivery, electronic warfare systems, navigation, communication and avionics integration.

Solid State Electronics Directorate is responsible for electronic device R&D for future AF systems needs in the areas of microelectronics, microwaves, and electro-optics. Research extends from fundamental semiconductor layer growth and device fabrication through analog and digital integrated circuits; also included is the computer-aided design software and work stations needed to pursue sample hybrid and monolithic integrated circuits.

Flight Dynamics Directorate pursues AF flight vehicle technologies to support aircraft, missiles and space systems in the technical areas of structures, vehicle subsystems, flight control, aeromechanics and experimental flight vehicle testbeds. Materials Directorate explores new materials and processes for advanced aerospace applications. Its current focus is on thermal protection materials, metallic and nonmetallic structural materials, aerospace propulsion materials, fluids and lubricants, electromagnetic and electronic materials and laser hardened materials.

Manufacturing Technology Directorate focuses on process technologies and integrated manufacturing. This directorate is responsible for a new initiative which integrates design and manufacturing technologies to stimulate a new focus on design for producibility, design for quality, and design for life cycle costs. Key elements of this concurrent engineering involve development of advanced tools in computer aided design and computer aided manufacturing for analyses of design for weapon performance and low cost manufacturing.

Plans and Programs Directorate is made up of cockpit integration, which involves research to advance the state of the art crew systems technologies for all classes of aerospace vehicles; and signature technology, which includes planning, formulating, and executing USAF exploratory and advanced development programs for vehicle signature reduction technology and counter low observable technology.

Armament Directorate develops conventional armament technology and integrates these technologies into air vehicle platforms and other delivery platforms. The directorate provides conventional armament technology for four major thrusts that include advanced guidance, weapon flight mechanics, ordnance, and conventional strategic defense.

AF Flight Test Center (AFFTC/BC)
(805)277-3900 x2275
5 South Wolfe Ave, Bldg 2800
Edwards AFB, CA 93524-1185
Principles interests: Test and evaluation of new and research aircraft. The center's contracting activity provides the contracting support necessary to accomplish the test mission and to provide operational support for base personnel/facilities, including the USAF Test Pilot School. Test mission procurements include telemetry equipment; flight test instrumentation; computer hardware and software; engineering, scientific and technical services, including management of the Edwards AFB Range; precision milling machines; aircraft maintenance; and radar components. Support to the test pilot school includes contracting for simulator training, glider training, and flight training/lectures. In addition, the AFFTC Contracting Center provides contracting support to the Propulsion Directorate of the Phillips Laboratory, a major tenant organization. Propulsion Directorate requirements include basic research, exploratory development and advanced development for strategic, tactical and space system propulsion.

The directorate also contracts for multiple space vehicle technologies including structures, structure dynamics, controls and power systems and is heavily involved in the Space Defense Initiative (SDI) program. The operational contracting division contracts for supplies, equipment, and work necessary for the operation and maintenance of Edwards AFB.

Electronic Systems Center (ESC/BC)
(617)377-4973
275 Randolph Rd
Hanscom AFB, MA 01731-2818

Principle interests: Plans and manages the acquisition and related engineering development of command, control, communications, and intelligence systems, subsystems and equipment including surveillance systems, navigation systems, air traffic control and landing systems, intelligence systems, electronic physical security surveillance and intrusion detection systems and weather systems, information and management systems until transfer of responsibility to the using command or agency. Evaluates using command requirements against available technology and potential costs and recommends necessary revisions. R&D contracts are also initiated by the Geophysics Division of the AF Laboratory in the environmental, physical and engineering sciences. The Geophysics Division performs research and exploratory and advanced Development in geophysics that is essential to the enhancement of AF operational capabilities. The work pursued may be categorized generally as falling within the following functional areas: Space Physics, Ionospheric Physics, Terrestrial

Science, Upper Atmospheric and Stratospheric operations, Optical/IR Backgrounds and Targets, Weather Specification and Prediction. Close liaison is maintained with AF operational elements, system development activities, and other AF laboratories, to identify research and technology needs and to accelerate the integration of scientific advances into AF technology. Geophysics Division carries out its assigned R&D mission responsibilities with in-house as well as contractual support.

While there are no AF aircraft assigned to Hanscom AFB, the operational contracting directorate does contract for all other work necessary for the operation and maintenance of the base.

Rome Laboratory (RL/BC)
(315)330-3311
26 Electronic Parkway
Griffis AFB, NY 13441-4514

Principle interests: AFMC laboratory specializing in the development of technologies for command, control, communications and intelligence systems. The laboratory's focus is to develop AF command and control systems, advanced computers and microchips, communication devices and techniques, software engineering, intelligence gathering and processing devices, surveillance systems, advanced radar, super conductivity, infrared sensors, cryogenics, artificial intelligence applications, and related technologies. It is the AF Center of Excellence in photonics research and the DoD focal point for reliability and compatibility.

AF Development Test Center (AFDTC/BC)
(904)882-2843
205 West D Ave, Ste 449
Eglin AFB, FL 32542-6863

Principles interests: Plans, directs, and conducts the test and evaluation of nonnuclear munitions, electronic combat, and navigation/ guidance systems. Related ASC System Program Offices (SPOs) are also located here and supported by AFDTC/BC. To accomplish this mission, AFDTC manages the large land test ranges that are located on the 724 square mile Eglin complex as well as the 86,500 square miles of water ranges located in the adjacent Gulf of Mexico. Major tests on or above AFDTC's ranges cover aircraft systems, subsystems, missiles, guns, rockets, targets and drones, high-powered radars, and electronic countermeasures equipment. AFDTC's unique assets include the Guided Weapons Evaluation Facility (GWEF), the Preflight Integration of Munitions and Electronic Systems (PRIMES),and the McKinley Climatic Laboratory, a facility capable of testing military hardware as large as aircraft in environments ranging from minus 65 to plus 165 degrees Fahrenheit with 100 mph winds,icing clouds, rain, and snow. AFDTC also is responsible for the 46th Test Group at Holloman AFB NM, with its high speed test track, two radar target scatter measurement facilities, and the Central Inertial Guidance Test Facility (CIGTF).

The operational contracting division contracts for supplies, equipment, and work necessary for the operation and maintenance of Eglin AFB.

Arnold Engineering Development Center (AEDC/BC)
(615)454-7841
100 Kindel Dr, Ste A332
Arnold AFB, TN 37389-1332

Principle interests: Provides aerodynamics R&D of power plants related to operation and test of air breathing propulsion systems (turbojet, ramjet, and turboprop); simulation of conditions of atmospheric, ballistic, orbital, and space flight; problems associated with high temperature materials; unique mechanical, electrical, and thermodynamic problems related to the construction of wind tunnels; high altitude propulsion test cells; space simulation chambers; impact and ballistic ranges and research units. Procurements include pumps and compressors (axial); compressors (centrifugal), rotors, and diffusers; high pressure airducting; wind tunnel accessories; test instrumentation; electromagnetic generators; test facility construction and modernization; high speed cameras; high temperature materials, cores, and bricks; architectural engineering services; ADP equipment; laboratory equipment; shop machinery.

Air Force Civil Engineering Center
(904)882-2843
Support Agency
Tyndall AFB, FL 32401

Principal interests: Contracts for the Air Force Engineering Service Center (AFESC). AFESC conducts planning, engineering development, investigative/applications engineering, and specialized civil engineering functions to enhance the technology and capabilities of AF civil engineering. The Center's capability complements the integral capabilities of major air commands, base level civil engineering organizations, and the civil engineering R&D community. The Center manages applied technology programs and introduces new technology into civil engineering operations through translation of state of the art research into usable systems, hardware, and techniques. Specific programs and areas of interest are mobility shelters; pre-engineered and relocatible facilities; modular facilities; snow and ice removal equipment and materials; corrosion abatement techniques and materials; fire/crash rescue equipment and materials; and other facilities, equipment materials, and techniques with potential application to the overall AF civil engineering area.

AF Office of Scientific Research (AFOSR/PK) (202)767-4946
110 Duncan Ave, Ste B115
Bolling AFB, DC 20332-8050

Principle interests: Encourages and supports fundamental research designed to increase the understanding of the natural sciences and to stimulate the recognition of new scientific concepts. Particularly desired are original and unique scientific approaches likely to clarify or extend understanding of the sciences which are of interest to the principal technical directorates of AFOSR. The AFOSR scientific directorates and areas of interest are:

Directorate Of Aerospace And Material Sciences (NA)
(202)767-4987
Structural mechanics; mechanics of materials; particulate mechanics; external aerodynamics and hypersonics; turbulence and internal flows; airbreathing combustion; space power and propulsion; metallic structural materials; ceramics and nonmetallic structural materials; organic matrix composites.

Directorate Of Physics And Electronics (NE)
(202)767-4985
Electromagnetic devices; novel electronic components, optoelectronic information processing: devices and systems; quantum electronic solids; semiconductor materials; electromagnetic materials; photonic physics; optics; atomic and molecular physics; plasma physics; imaging physics.

Directorate Of Chemistry And Life Sciences (NL)
(202)767-5021
Chemical reactivity and synthesis; polymer chemistry; surface science; theoretical-chemistry molecular dynamics; chronobiology and neural adaptation; perception and cognition; sensory systems; bioenvironmental sciences.

Directorate Of Mathematics And Geosciences (NM)
(202)767-5025
Dynamics and controls; physical mathematics and applied analysis; computational mathematics; optimization and discrete mathematics; signal processing, probability, and statistics; software and systems; artificial intelligence; electromagnetic; meteorology; atmospheric sciences; space sciences.

Directorate Of Academic And International Affairs (NI)
(202)767-8073

Sponsors researcher assistance programs that stimulate scientific and engineering education and increase the interaction between the broader research community and the Air Force laboratories.

The directorate is also responsible for managing the Small Business Innovative Research (SBIR) and the Small Business Technology Transfer (STTR) programs for AFOSR. Specific research topics are selected for each solicitation. Industrial concerns and nonprofit organization having research capabilities in major scientific fields, and those whose personnel include competent scientific investigators, may submit basic research proposals. General questions about the Department of Defense SBIR/STTR programs should be referred to the SBIR/STTR Help Desk at (800)382-4634. AFOSR specific questions should be referred to the SBIR/STTR program manager in AFOSR/NI, (202)767-6962.

New World Vistas
AFOSR is specifically, but not exclusively, interested in sponsoring basic research that supports the science and technology areas identified in the Air Force Scientific Advisory board's New World Vistas report. The New World Vistas report identifies science and technology needed to support six future Air Force capability areas. The Air Force intends to invest in basic research that supports some or all of these subareas in the near future.

Global Awareness
(202)767-7899
Network data fusion for global awareness; lightweight antenna structures; low-cost, lightweight membrane structures; in situ sensors; global awareness virtual testbed; low noise/high-uniformity broadband sensors.

Dynamic Planning And Execution Control
(202)767-7899
Planning and scheduling; communications; knowledge bases; intelligent agents for Air Force battlefield and enterprise information assistants; information warfare; new models of computation; domain-specific component-based software development.

Global Mobility In War And Peace
(202)767-0467
Precision air delivery; composite materials and structures; low-specific-fuel-consumption propulsion; aerodynamics and controls subsystems integration/power; advanced landing gear; microelectromechanical systems; active defense systems; battlefield awareness/weather predictions; human systems interface and training.

Projection Of Lethal And Sublethal Power
(202)767-0467
Uninhabited aerial vehicles; hypersonics; lethal andsublethal directed-energy weapons; energy-coupling modeling and simulation.

Space Operations
(202)767-4984
Microsatellites; distributed functionality; precision deployable large antennas/optics; high efficiency electrical laser sources; space object identification and orbit prediction; high-energy-density propellants; jam-proof, area-deniable propagation; nanosecond global clock accuracy; hypervelocity dynamics; low-cost, lightweight structures and materials; power generation and storage.

People
(202)767-4278
Human-machine interface; team decision making; cognitive engineering.

ADVANCED RESEARCH PROJECTS AGENCY

The Advanced Research Projects Agency (ARPA) is the central research and development organization for the Department of Defense (DoD). It manages and directs selected basic and applied research and development projects for DoD, and pursues research and technology where risk and payoff are both very high and where success may provide dramatic advances for traditional military roles and missions and dual-use applications.

ARPA's primary responsibility is to help maintain U.S. technological superiority and guard against unforeseen technological advances by potential adversaries. Consequently, the ARPA mission is to develop imaginative, innovative, and often high risk research ideas offering a significant technological impact that will go well beyond the normal evolutionary developmental approaches; and to pursue these ideas from the demonstration of technical feasibility through the development of prototype systems.

The challenge of the ARPA mission is met by a small group of technical program managers with flexibility for quick implementation of R&D initiatives. The current ARPA Technical Program has been organized around the following major thrusts, selected because of their importance to national defense and dual-use applications.

- Technology Reinvestment Project
- High Performance Computing
- Advanced Simulation
- Smart Weapons
- Microelectronics Production Technology

· Joint Biomedical Technology Program
· Acoustic Warfare and Submarine Stealth
· Software and Intelligent Systems
· Advanced Satellite Technology
· Special Materials

Entities seeking R&D support from ARPA should explore the Agency's interests in research by reviewing sources such as the Commerce Business Daily (CBD), open literature, published testimony before Congressional committees, and the Department of Defense Small Business Innovation Research (SBIR) Program Solicitation. Inquiries regarding ARPA technologies may be addressed to:

Director
Advanced Research Projects Agency
(703) 696-2448
3701 North Fairfax Drive
ATTN: OASB
Arlington, VA 22203-1714

Defense Technical Information Center
(703) 767-8226
ATTN: DTIC, Suite 0944 Toll-free:
8725 John J. Kingman Road (outside DC area)
Fort Belvoir, VA 22060-6218 1 (800) DOD SBIR

DoD's central facility for the distribution of scientific and technical reports generated by defense-funded efforts in virtually all areas of R&D; operates computer-based data bank of management and technical information and is responsible for the development of information storage and retrieval systems. Data banks cover the past, present, and future defense R&D programs. The services offered are available to defense and other federal activities and to all their contractors, subcontractors, and grantees.

GUIDE FOR PREPARING UNSOLICITED PROPOSALS

An unsolicited proposal is a written proposal independently originated and developed by the offeror and submitted to DoD for the purpose of obtaining a contract. To be considered for acceptance, an unsolicited proposal must be innovative and unique and in sufficient detail to allow a determination that DoD support would benefit the agency's mission responsibilities. An unsolicited proposal is not a response to an agency request or an advance proposal for an agency requirement that could be met by competitive methods.

There is no particular format to be followed in preparation of unsolicited proposals. Elaborate proposals are discouraged. The proposal should contain the following information to permit consideration in an objective and timely manner:

Basic Information. Offeror's name, address, and type of organization; e.g., profit, nonprofit, educational, small business, minority business, women-owned business.

Names and telephone numbers of technical and business personnel to be contacted for evaluation or negotiation purposes.

Names of other Federal, State, and local agencies, or other parties, if any, receiving the proposal or funding the proposed effort.

Date of submission and signature of a person authorized to represent and contractually obligate the offeror.

Technical Information. A concise, descriptive title and an abstract (200-300 words) stating the basic purpose, summary of work, and expected end result of the proposed effort.

A reasonably complete narrative in which the relevance of the proposed work to the DoD mission is discussed. State the problems to be addressed; the specific objectives of the research, and the expected consequences of successful completion of the research, including potential economic and other benefits.

Provide a full and complete description of the work to be performed, the method of approach, and the extent of effort to be employed. Indicate an estimated period of time in which to accomplish the objectives, and criteria by which success of the project can be evaluated.

Names and biographical information on the key personnel who would be involved in the project.

Any support needed from the agency; e.g., facilities, equipment, material.

Supporting Information. A breakdown of the proposed cost or price in sufficient detail for meaningful evaluation. Show the estimated cost of materials and how you established it. Show the estimated costs of labor by category (engineering, manufacturing, test, etc.) and show the salary rates for each category. Show the indirect expense rates (manufacturing and engineering overheads, general and administrative expenses) to be applied. Explain the basis for the labor and indirect expense rates included in your cost breakdown (e.g., current experienced rates, projected from current experience, budgetary, etc.). Identify and explain the basis for any other cost elements included in your proposal.

A statement as to the proposed duration of the effort, the type of contract preferred, and the length of time for which the proposal is valid (a 6 month minimum is suggested).

A brief description of any previous or ongoing R&D work performed in the field or in related fields. Describe briefly the facilities and any special equipment available to perform the proposed effort.

Unsolicited proposals may include proprietary data which the offeror does not want disclosed to the public or used by the Government for any purpose other than proposal evaluation. DoD cannot assume responsibility for use of such data unless it is specifically and clearly marked with the following legend on the title page:

Use and Disclosure of Data
The data in this proposal shall not be disclosed outside the Government and shall not be duplicated, used, or disclosed in whole or in part for any purpose other than to evaluate the proposal; provided that if a contract is awarded to the offeror as a result of or in connection with the submission of these data, the Government shall have the right to duplicate, use, or disclose the data to the extent provided in the contract. This restriction does not limit the Government's right to use information contained in the data if it is obtainable from another source without restriction. The data subject to this restriction are contained in Sheets _____. Each restricted sheet should be marked with the following legend: "Use or disclosure of proposal data is subject to the restriction on the title page of this proposal."

Chapter 4:

SPECIAL PURCHASING OFFICES

There are three categories of goods and services which are purchased by special purchasing offices. These are merchandise for defense commissary stores, resale merchandise for the military exchange services, and motion pictures and videotape production.

The Defense Commissary Agency (DeCA)

DeCA Is a chain of supermarkets (commissaries) providing quality goods at the lowest possible cost to authorized patrons. We have three regional offices in the United States and one in Europe. For more information see website http://www.commissaries.com.

DeCA Is Not associated with any other military resale or retail activity. Other entities operate and manage these activities known as club systems, ship stores, or exchanges. DeCA is also not associated with dining facilities (mess halls, dining halls, galleys, etc.). The dining facilities are operated by the individual Armed Services to provide prepared meals for their members.

What DeCA Buys
Grocery Products-- Our resale products are those traditionally sold in commercial supermarkets. Commodities and products sold in the commissaries are restricted to those authorized by the U.S. Congress. (See the "Resale" section for more information.)

Operational Support-- Equipment, supplies and services required to support the operation of individual commissaries (stores).

Administrative Support - Supplies and services to support the overall operation of the Agency.

DeCA has a preference for commercial type products.

Resale Focus
Resale includes both brand name and non-brand name products. Brand name products are those that have identifiable customer recognition, and are marketed, merchandised and commercially available and sold based on that brand. We carry these products because the commissary patron prefers the brand name. Non-brand name products are products for which there is no customer preference and include meat, eggs, etc. and in-store resale operations (deli/bakery). They are procured competitively using commercial descriptions. (See the "Resale" section for more information.)

Other Than Resale Focus

Other than resale means operational and administrative support items as defined above. (See the "Operational and Administrative Support Items" section for more information.) These acquisitions account for less than 5 percent of DeCA's total contractual awards.

Your Market Key for Brand Name Items

The first step in selling us a brand name product is to make an item presentation to one of our buyers. The presentation is your opportunity to market your product and provide any unique information. Before selection, a brand name product must have a universal product code (UPC) and be sold in commercial supermarkets. For more information regarding product UPC, you can contact Uniform Code Council Inc. at (937) 435-3870 or see web cite http://www.uc-council.org . Details of your offer must be summarized on DeCA Form 40-33, Item Presentation Form, which may be obtained from a local commissary or from one of the points of contact under the "Getting Started" section.

For brand name resale items, your product's performance determines whether it remains in our stock assortment. We continuously analyze product sales information and if sales trends indicate your product is moving, then replenishment quantities are ordered; if not, your product will be removed from our shelves. Specific time frames for measuring product performance will be explained during your presentation.

Products for national distribution are normally presented at our corporate headquarters at Fort Lee, VA. Products with regional or local distribution may be presented at one of our region offices or an individual commissary. Our small business specialists, category managers, or region buyers can help you decide which location is best for your presentation.

Points of Contact/DeCA Headquarters /Ft Lee

LOCATION	TOPIC	NAME	TELEPHONE
Acquisition Management (AM)	Small Business	General Information	(804) 734-8740 Internet E-Mail (smallbus@hqlee.deca.mil)
Contract Management Business Unit (CBU)	Operational Items	Small Business Specialist	(804) 734-8255
nformation Management (IM)	Electronic Data Interchange (EDI)	Jeffrey Perry, EDI Coordinator	(804) 734-8482 Internet E-mail (perryjc@hqlee.deca.mil)
	Resale Items	Perishable Market	(804) 734-9979

Marketing Business Unit (MBU)	Resale Items	Perishable Market	(804) 734-9979
		Semi-Perishable Market	(804) 734-9980
		Local/Regional Buying	(804) 734-9947

DeCA Region Locations and Points of Contact

REGION	LOCATION	AREA COVERED
Eastern Region	5151 Bonney Road, Suite 201 Virginia Beach, VA 23462-4314	
Northern Area Office	2257 Huber Rd Fort Meade, Md 20755-5220 Small Bus Spec* (301) 677-9893 Resale (301) 677-9265	Maine, New Hampshire, Vermont, Rhode Island Massachusetts, Connecticut, New York, New Jersey, Pennsylvania, Maryland, Delaware, Virginia, West Virginia, Kentucky, Missouri, Ohio, Washington DC,
Southern Area Office	60 West Maxwell Blvd. Maxwell AFB, AL 36112-6307 Small Bus Spec* (334) 953-3136 Resale (334) 953-7795	Illinois, Indiana, Wisconsin, Minnesota, Michigan, Iowa, Arkansas, Tennessee, North Carolina, Louisiana, Mississippi, Alabama, Georgia, South Carolina, Florida, Caribbean and Central America
Midwest Region	300 AFCOMS Way Kelly AFB, TX 78241-6132 Small Bus Spec* (210) 925-5924 Resale (210) 925-6459	North Dakota, South Dakota, Wyoming, Kansas, Oklahoma, New Mexico, Texas, Colorado, Nebraska
Western/Pacific Region	3401 Beech Street McClellan AFB, CA 95652-1164 (916) 643-0222 - Small Bus Spec* (916) 569-4827 – Resale	Washington, Oregon, Idaho, Montana, California, Utah, Arizona, Alaska, Hawaii, Far East, Nevada
European Region	Gebaude 2780, Zimmer 109,	Germany, United Kingdom,

Kapun AS,
67661 Vogelweh/Kaiserslautern
GE
011-49-0631-3523-105 Resale
Small Business Specialist

Italy, Greece, Turkey, The
Netherlands, Belgium Spain,
Azores, Saudi Arabia, Egypt

Defense Commissary Agency
Acquisition Management
1300 E Avenue, Building 11200
Fort Lee, Virginia 23801-1800
(804) 734-8740

MILITARY EXCHANGE SERVICES

The categories of merchandise and price limitations on goods sold by military exchange services in the continental United States are established by regulations approved by Congress. These limitations do not apply to overseas exchanges.

The buying offices and procedures for dealing with the exchanges are set forth below.

Army and Air Force Exchange Service

To sell to the Army and Air Force Exchange Service a firm must offer its product to the appropriate buyer at the Headquarters or the exchange region office. No merchandise is purchased by individual exchanges. The Headquarters buyers purchase all resale merchandise that is commonly stocked in post and base exchanges in the CONUS, and all resale merchandise of United States origin for overseas exchanges. Merchandise peculiar to single exchange regions is purchased by these four exchange regional offices, each of which has approximately 36 exchanges located in its geographical area.

Central Region
Army and Air Force
Exchange Service
P. O. Box 650454
Dallas, TX 75265-0454
(972) 277-7203

Eastern Region
Army and Air Force Service
P. O. Box 650455
Dallas, TX 75265-0455
(972) 277-7103

Southern Region
Army and Air Force
Exchange Service
P. O. Box 65044
Dallas, TX 75265-0447
(972) 277-7300

Western Region
Army and Air Force
Exchange Service
P. O. Box 650429
Dallas, TX 75265-0429
(972) 277-7403

The Navy Exchange Program

The Navy Exchange Program is a Navy retailing operation that provides quality products and a variety of services to the men and women of the Armed Forces, with special emphasis on serving members of the U.S. Navy and their families. Navy Exchanges are located at U.S. Navy bases in the United States and in 19 countries around the world.

Navy Exchanges are self-supporting and do not receive tax dollars for their operation. Net profits generated by Navy Exchange sales are returned to Navy bases to help support local and Navy-wide recreation and morale programs. These include such on-base activities as physical fitness centers; swimming pools; child care centers; libraries; intramural sports programs; special entertainment events and other activities. Please note that additional information on the Navy and Marine Exchange program can be found by accessing the World Wide Web at: http://www.navy-nex.com.

Navy Exchanges

Navy Exchanges consist of retail and services departments and are operated in a similar manner to commercial retail enterprises, within limitations established by Congress and the Department of Defense. Exchanges provide basic staple merchandise and a selection of other items to meet the needs of authorized customers. There are 133 Navy Exchanges worldwide.

Services available to authorized Navy exchange customers include: automotive service centers; fast food outlets; snack bars; cafeterias, food carts, mobile canteens; laundry and dry cleaning; vending machines; optical shops; photo finishing, specialty stores; barber and beauty salons; flower shops; video and car rental; and other personalized services.

Contacting NEXCOM Buyers

The NEXCOM Command maintains an open door policy in meeting with all potential suppliers. Open Vendor Day is held the first Wednesday of each month for those vendors who are not currently doing business with the Navy Exchange System. Sales personnel are invited to call the appropriate buyer to schedule an appointment. Appointments are taken on a first-come, first-serve basis between 9:00 am - 3:00 p.m.

Inquiries and correspondence should be directed to a retail or services buyer at the address below:

Navy Exchange Service Command
3280 Virginia Beach Boulevard
Virginia Beach, VA 23452-5724
Phone: 757-631-6200

The Small Business Office provides information about how to go about doing business with the Navy Exchange System. The small business specialist can be contacted at 804-631-3582.

The locations of NEXCOMs and the Navy Exchanges that each supports is shown in the following list: (Numbers in parenthesis show the number of Navy exchanges in that particular area):

NEXCEN Norfolk
Eastern/Tidewater
Area
Navy Exchange
Service Command
3280 Virginia Beach
Command
Virginia Beach, VA
23452-5724
Phone: 757-440-4500
Fax: 757-440-4526

NEXCEN Norfolk Exchanges

Lakehurst, NJ	Colts Neck, NJ
Brunswick, ME	Cutler, ME
Newport, RI	Winter Harbor, ME
Norfolk, VA (3)	Portsmouth, VA (2)
Oceana, VA	Chesapeake, VA
Yorktown, VA	Dahlgren, VA
Dam Neck, VA	Little Creek, VA
Patuxent River, MD	Annapolis, MD
Indian Head, MD	Bethesda, MD
Washington, DC	Sugar Grove, WV
Philadelphia, PA (2)	Willow Grove, PA
Arlington, VA	Bermuda
South Weymouth, MA	Mechanicsburg, PA
Mitchel Field, NY	Warminister, PA
Portsmouth, NH	Scotia, NY
Keflavik, Iceland	New London, CT

Cheltenham,
MD

NEXCEN Jacksonville
Southern/Florida Area
Navy Exchange
Service Center
Box 13
Naval Air Station
Jacksonville, FL 32212
Phone: 904-777-7075
Fax: 904-777-7008

NEXCEN Jacksonville Exchanges

Jacksonville, FL	Key West, FL
Mayport, FL	Cecil Field, FL
Orlando, FL	Athens, GA
Kings Bay, GA	Beaufort, SC
Charleston, SC (2)	Antigua
Roosevelt Roads, PR	Guantanamo Bay, Cuba
Sabana Seca, PR	

NEXCEN San Diego
California/Pacific
Northwest
Navy Exchange
Service Center
Naval Station, Box
368150
San Diego, CA 92136-
5150
Phone: 619-237-5601
Fax: 619-237-5609

NEXCEN San Diego Exchanges

Concord, CA	Coronado, CA
San Diego, CA (4)	Stockton, CA
San Nicholas, CA	Treasure Island, CA
Port Hueneme, CA	Hamilton-Novato, CA
China Lake, CA	Alameda, CA (2)
El Centro, CA	Mare Island, CA
Imperial Beach, CA	Oakland, CA (2)
Long Beach, CA	Ferndale, CA
Miramar, CA	Lemoore, CA
North Island, CA (2)	Moffett Field, CA
Point Mugu,	Monterey, CA

CA

Fallon, NV	Bangor, WA
Bremerton, WA	Everett, WA
Smokey Point, WA	Whidbey Island, WA

NEXCEN Pearl Harbor
Hawaii Area
Navy Exchange
Service Center
Box 133
Pearl Harbor, HI 96860
Phone: 808-423-3201
Fax: 808-422-7897

NEXCEN Pearl Harbor Exchanges

Barbers Point, HI	Pearl Harbor, HI
Kauai, HI	Wahiawa, HI
Laulualei, HI	Christchurch, New Zealand

Independent
Exchanges - Domestic
Great Lakes, Illinois
Navy Exchange
2701 Sheridan Rd.,
Building 111
Naval Training Center
Great Lakes, IL 60085-5129
Phone: 847-578-6103
Fax: 847-578-6301

Great Lakes Exchanges

Glenview, IL	Crane, IN
Great Lakes, IL (2)	

Pensacola, Florida
Navy Exchange
Naval Air Station
250 Chamber Ave.
Pensacola, FL 60085-5129
Phone: 904-578-6100

Pensacola Exchanges

Pensacola, FL (2)	Meridian, MS
Panama City, FL	Gulfport, MS
Whiting Field, FL	New Orlean, LA
Pascagoula, MS	

Dallas, Texas
Navy Exchange
Naval Air Station
Dallas, TX 75211-9501

Memphis, Tennessee
Navy Exchange
Naval Air Station, Memphis
7800 3rd Avenue
Millington, TN 38054-6024

Phone: 214-266-6411 Phone: 901-872-7716
Fax: 214-266-6414 Fax: 901-872-7718

Corpus Christi, Texas Corpus Christi Exchanges
Navy Exchange Corpus Christi, TX
Naval Air Station Kingsville, TX
651 Lexington Blvd. Ingleside, TX
Corpus Christi, TX
78419
Phone: 512-939-2033
Fax: 512-939-8529

Independent Guam Guam Exchanges
Exchanges - Overseas Agana, Guam (3)
U.S. Navy Exchange Singapore
Guam
PSC 455, Box 178
FPO AP 96540-1000
Phone: 011-671-339-
3251
Fax: 011-671-564-
3215

Military Sealift Command (MSC) Exchanges

MSC Atlantic Area MSC Pacific Area
Commander, Military Sealift Commander, Military Sealift
Command Command
Military Ocean Terminal Naval Supply Center
Building 42, Room 4.131 Building 310-1E (Code
(code N43) N43)
Bayonne, NJ 07002-5399 Oakland, CA 94625-5010
Phone: 201-823-7615 or Phone: 510-302-6212 or
7479 6214
Fax: 201-823-6573 (ATTN: Fax: 510-302-6940 (ATTN:
Code N43) Code N43)

Navy Uniform Program
As program manager for Navy Uniforms, the Navy Uniform Program is the only
authorized source of certified Navy Uniforms. The Navy Uniform Program
encompasses the management of government issue uniform items.

Information regarding Navy Uniform procurement procedures, inquiries and correspondence should be directed to Ms. Becky Adkins, Director of Navy Uniforms, at the address and numbers listed below:

Navy Uniforms
1545 Crossways Boulevard
Suite 100
Chesapeake, VA 23320
Phone: 757-420-9116
Fax: 757-420-4094

Ships Store Program

To meet the needs of the afloat sailor, ships stores carry basic toiletries and sundries, high demand items such as soft drinks and candy bars, and "nice to have" items which include consumer electronics merchandise. The limited cube and space on board each ship restricts selection to those items that are the most popular. However, sailors have the ability to special order almost any item a Navy Exchange carries. The Ship's Supply Officer or an appointed Ships Store Officer supervises and initiates the purchasing for the ships store based on the crew's needs and inventory limitations using the Ships Store Afloat Catalogs (SSAC), Contract Bulletins or by initiating a special purchase order. Inquiries and correspondence should be directed to the Director of Ship Stores Program, at the address and numbers listed below:

Ship Stores Program
3280 Virginia Beach Boulevard
Virginia Beach, VA 23452
Phone: 757-445-6899
Fax: 757-445-6920

The Marine Corps Exchange Program

Marine Corps Morale, Welfare and Recreation (MWR) is a diverse collection of activities, services, and programs which support the quality of life of the Marine Corps community, active duty, reserves and retired.

Marine Corps Market Points of Contact

MCLB Barstow, CA	HQMC, HQBN Arlington,
MWR Director	Virginia
Marine Corps Logistics	MWR Director
Base	Headquarters Battalion
Building 44	Henderson Hall
Barstow, CA 92311-5018	Arlington, VA 22214-5003
Phone: 619-577-6733	Phone: 703-979-0972 Ext. 324
MCAGCC Twentynine	MCCDC Quantico, Virginia

Palms, CA
MWR Director
Marine Corps Air Ground
Combat Center
Box 788150
Twentynine Palms, CA
92278-8150
Phone: 619-830-6870

MWR Director
Marine Corps Base
Building 2034
Quantico, VA 22134-5000
Phone: 703-784-3007

MCAS El Toro/Tustin, CA
MWR Director
Marine Corps Air Bases
West
Building 75
Marine Corps Air Station El
Toro
Santa Ana, CA 92709-5018
Phone: 714-726-2571

MCSFBN, Norfolk, Virginia
MWR Director
MCSFBN
1320 Piercy Street
Norfolk, VA 23511
Phone: 757-423-1187

MCB Camp Pendleton, CA
MWR Director
Marine Corps Base
P. O. Box 555020
Camp Pendleton, CA
92055-5020
Phone: 619-725-5551

MCAS Cherry Point, NC
MWR Director
PSC Box 8009
Marine Corps Air Station
Building 400
Cherry Point, NC 28533-809
Phone: 919-466-2430

MCRD San Diego, CA
MWR Director
Marine Corps Recruit
Depot/WRR
Building 10
San Diego, CA 92140-5196
Phone: 619-524-4433

MCB Camp Lejeune, North
Carolina
MWR Director
Marine Corps Base
Building 1
Camp Lejeune, NC 28542-
5001
Phone: 910-451-2524

MCAS Yuma, AZ
MWR Director
Marine Corps Air Station
Building 633
Yuma, AZ 85369-5000
Phone: 520-341-3531

MCAS New River, North
Carolina
MWR Director
Marine Corps Air Station,
New River
Building 208
Jacksonville, NC 8545-5001

MCAS Beaufort, South
Carolina
MWR Director
Marine Corps Air Station
Building 408

MCAS Iwakuni, Japan
MWR Director
Marine Corps Air Station,
Iwakuni
PSC 561, Box 1867

Beaufort, SC 29904-5003
Phone: 803-522-7572

MCRD Parris Island, South
Carolina
MWR Director
Marine Corps Recruit
Depot/ERR
Building 202
P. O. Box 5100
Parris Island, SC 29905-
5003
Phone: 803-525-3301

MCLB Albany, Georgia
MWR Director
Marine Corps Logistics
Base
814 Radford Boulevard
Building 7520
Albany, GA 31704-1128
Phone: 912-439-5267

MCB Hawaii
MWR Director
Marine Corps Base Hawaii
Building 1404
Kaneohe Bay, HI 96863-
5018
Phone: 808-254-7500

FPO AP 96310-1867
Fax: 011-81-827-21-4181

MCB Camp Butler,
Okinawa, Japan
MWR Director
Marine Corps Base Camp
Butler
Unit 35023
FPO AP 96373-5023
Fax: 011-81-98-893-8329

MCAS Kansas City,
Missouri
MWR Director
Richards-Gebaur
Marine Corps Support
Activity
1500 East Bannister Road
Kansas City, MO 64197-
0501
Phone: 816-843-3800

MCAS Guantanamo Bay,
Cuba
MWR Director
Marine Barracks
U. S. Naval Base,
Guantanamo Bay, Cuba
Box 32
FPO AE 09596-0120
Fax: 011-53-99-3237

COMPUTER SYSTEMS
Activities Involved in Procurement of ADPE, Software, Maintenance and Services

Department of the Army
CECOM Acquisition Center
Navy Information System and
Acquisition Agency
Washington Operation Office
2461 Eisenhower Ave.
Alexandria, VA 22331-0700
Tel: (703) 325-5793

Department of the Army
Defense Supply Service-
Washington
5200 Army Pentagon
Washington, DC 20310-5210
Tel: (703) 697-6024

CECOM - Acquisition Center
ATTN: AMSEL-IE-SB
Fort Huachuca, AZ 85613-5000
Tel: (520) 538-7870

Department of Air Force
Electronic System Division
275 Randolph Road
Hanscom AFB, MA 01731-
5000
Tel: (617) 377-4973

SSC/PK
375 Libby Street
Maxwell AFB
Gunter Annex, AL 36114-3207
Tel: (334) 416-5614

Defense Logistics Agency

Department of the Navy
Management Center
Code OOX1, Bldg. 176-4
Washington Navy Yard
Washington, DC 20374-
5070
Tel: (202) 433-4337

Naval Fleet and Industrial
Supply Center
Long Beach Detachment
Code, PA, Bldg. 53, 2nd
Floor
Long Beach, CA 90822-
5074
Tel: (310) 901-3794

Naval Fleet and Industrial
Supply Center
Washington Navy Yard,
Building 200
901 M Street S. E., Code
OOA
Washington, DC 20374-
2000
Tel: (202) 433-2957

Naval Fleet and Industrial
Supply Center
Code 09B
Philadelphia Detachment
Philadelphia, PA 19112-
5083
Tel: (215) 697-9555

Defense Information
System Agency
701 South Courthouse
Road
Arlington, VA 22204-
2199
Tel: (703) 607-6920

Administrative Support Center
Office of Contracting
ATTN: Deputy for Small
Business
8725 John J. Kingman Road
Suite 0119, Room 1134
Fort Belvoir, VA 22206-6220
Tel: (703) 767-1161

MOTION PICTURE AND VIDEOTAPE PRODUCTIONS

Motion picture and videotape productions are purchased only from qualified producers. To obtain an application form for acceptance on the Qualified Film Producers List or the Qualified Videotape Producers List, contact the Joint Visual Information Activity Office, 601 North Fairfax Street, Room 334, Alexandria, Virginia 22314-2007, telephone (703) 428-0636. They serve as an executive agent for all Federal agencies, including the Department of Defense. To become qualified, producers submit sample films or videotapes to a review board. Ultimately, contracts are placed by authorized procurement offices of the Army, Navy and Air Force. In order for a producer to receive a contract from an authorized procurement office, the producer must first be approved for the appropriate qualified list.

Note that audiovisual services such as processing or graphics, and audiovisual equipment are purchased by the requiring post, camp, station, or installation.

Authorized Military Service procurement offices are:

Army
Joint Visual Information Activity Washington - Contracting
601 N. Fairfax Street, Room 334
Alexandria, VA 22314-2007
703-428-1122

Joint Visual Information Activity - Production
601 N. Fairfax Street, Room 334
Alexandria, VA 22314-2007
703-248-1118

Navy and Marine Corps
Navy Imaging Command
Anacostia Naval Station
Production Contracting Department
Building 168
Washington, DC 20374-1681
(202) 433-5775

Chapter 5:

BUYING PROPERTY FROM THE U.S. GOVERNMENT

The Federal Government sells large quantities of many kinds of real and personal property including critical and strategic materials which become surplus to its needs.

Surplus personal property normally is sold on a competitive bid basis to the highest acceptable bidder. Most sales are made by sealed bids solicited by the selling office. Some sales are effected by auction or by spot bid sales. Military surplus personal property is marketed by the Defense Reutilization and Marketing Service. Civilian surplus personal property is sold by GSA personal property sales offices, each of which maintain its own bidders lists.

Surplus real property generally is advertised for sale by GSA on a competitive bid basis. Land and improvements held by the Departments of Defense, Agriculture, and Interior that have a value of less than $1,000 are offered for sale by these Departments. Otherwise the sales are made through the GSA Real Property Sales Offices which widely publicizes scheduled sales.

DEFENSE REUTILIZATION AND MARKETING SERVICE

The Defense Reutilization and Marketing Service (DRMS) of the Defense Logistics Agency is responsible for managing the Department of Defense (DoD) Government Sales Program. Excess personal property from U.S. military units is turned over to more that 190 Defense Reutilization and Marketing Offices (DRMOs) located on major military installations around the world. The property is first looked at for reutilization or reuse within DoD. When property cannot be reused, it is offered for transfer or donation to other Federal agencies and qualified state and local agencies. The remaining property is declared surplus and offered for sale to the public.

Property varies in type and value and includes tents, typewriters, computers, vehicles, aircraft components and accessories, engine accessories, office furniture and equipment, clothing, household paints and thinners, recyclable materials such as iron, aluminum, copper, paper, and much more. DRMS does not sell real estate.

DoD Government Surplus Sales are held at DRMOs which are designed similar to a local retail store where property is offered at a fixed price. All property is sold "As Is, Where Is." The method of payment is "cash and carry." The buyers pay for merchandise and remove the property at the time of sale.

National International Sales are conducted by the DRMS International Sales Office in Memphis, TN, and includes: international auctions; sealed bids, which allow bidders to enter their written bids during a specified time; and negotiated sales in certain circumstances. International sales include such items as aircraft, ships, hazardous property having wide commercial applications.

FOR MORE INFORMATION:
To request the free booklet "How to Buy Surplus Personal Property from DoD", which lists the DRMS regional offices worldwide and includes almost 20 categories of goods, call 1(888)352-9333, or see the DRMS Home Page, at http://www.drms.dla.mil .

If you are interested in local sales, call 1(800)-GOVT BUY to obtain the phone number of your nearest DRMO.

If you are interested in National/international sales, call 1(888)352-9333 or write the International Sales Office, 2163 Airways Blvd., Memphis, TN 38114-5211.

GSA REGIONAL PERSONAL PROPERTY SALES OFFICES (More information can be obtained through the World Wide Web on http://www.gsa.gov).

WASHINGTON, DC, METROPOLITAN AREA
Chief, Personal Property Program
470 L' Enfant Plaza, Suite 8214
Washington, DC 20407
(703) 557-7796

SAN FRANCISCO, CALIFORNIA
American Samoa, Arizona, California, Guam, Hawaii, and Nevada
Property Management Branch
450 Golden Gate Ave., West Side
P.O. Box 36018
San Francisco, CA 94102-3400
(415) 522-2891 or 1(800) 676-7253

DENVER, COLORADO
Colorado, Montana, North Dakota, South Dakota, Utah, Wyoming
Property Management Branch
Denver Federal Center, Bldg. 41
P.O. Box 25506
Denver, CO 80225-0506
(202)236-7705

ATLANTA, GEORGIA
Alabama, Florida, Georgia, Kentucky, Mississippi, North Carolina, South Carolina, and Tennessee,
Property Management Branch
401 West Peachtree Street
Atlanta, GA 30365-2550
(404) 331-5177, ext. 100

CHICAGO, ILLINOIS
Illinois, Indiana, Michigan, Minnesota, Ohio, Wisconsin
Property Management Branch
230 South Dearborn Street
Chicago, IL 60604
(312)353-0246

BOSTON, MASSACHUSETTS
Connecticut, Maine, Massachusetts, New Hampshire, Rhode Island, Vermont
Property Management Branch
10 Causeway Street
3rd Floor, Room 347
Boston, MA 0222-1076
(617)565-7326

KANSAS, CITY, MISSOURI
Iowa, Kansas, Missouri, Nebraska
Property Management Branch
1500 East Bannister Road
Room 1102
Kansas City, MO 64131

NEW YORK, NEW YORK
New Jersey, New York, Puerto Rico, Virgin Islands
Property Management Branch
Room 20-112, Box 10
26 Federal Plaza
New York, NY 10278
(212)264-4823 or 1(800) 488-7253

PHILADELPHIA, PENNSYLVANIA
Delaware, Maryland and Virginia, Pennsylvania, West Virginia
Property Management Branch
Wanamaker Building
100 Penn Square East
Philadelphia, PA 19107-3396

FORT WORTH, TEXAS
Arkansas, Louisiana, New Mexico, Oklahoma, and Texas
Property Management Branch
819 Taylor Street
Fort Worth, TX 76102-6105
(817) 978-2352 or 1(800) 495-1276

DEFENSE NATIONAL STOCKPILE CENTER
The Defense National Stockpile Center (DNSC) of the Defense Logistics Agency is responsible for managing the nation's reserves of strategic and critical materials for times of national emergency. Procures and sells aluminum, beryllium, cobalt, germanium, lead, manganese, mercury, mica, and rubber. To obtain further information on doing business with the Defense National Stockpile Center, call (703) 767-6500 or visit the DNSC Home Page at https://www.dnsc.dla.mil

Chapter 6:

OFFICES PROVIDING ASSISTANCE TO SMALL BUSINESSES FOR DEFENSE PROCUREMENT

DEFENSE CONTRACT MANAGEMENT COMMANDS (DCMCs)

The contract management commands can help you find subcontracting opportunities and assist you in identifying DoD contracting offices likely to buy your products or services. The DCMCs are not buying offices and therefore SF 129s should not be sent to these activities.

EAST

DCMD East
495 Summer Street
Boston, MA 02210-2184
(617) 753-4317 or 4318
Toll Free: (800) 321-1861

DCMC Atlanta
805 Walker Street
Marietta, GA 30060-2789
(770) 590-6197/6418
Toll Free: (800) 932-3561

DCMC Baltimore
200 Towsontown Blvd.,
Towson, MD 21204-5299
(410) 339-4809

DCMC Birmingham
West Burger Phillips Centre
1910 3rd Ave., North, Rm. 201
Birmingham, AL 35203-3502
(205) 716-7403

DCMC Boston
495 Summer Street
Boston, MA 02210-2184
(617) 753-3467/4110

DCMC Clearwater
Gadsden Building
9549 Koger Blvd., Suite 200
St. Petersburg, FL 33702-2455
(813) 579-3093

DCMC Cleveland
555 E. 88th Street
Cleveland, OH 44199-2064
(330) 522-5446/6582

DCMC Dayton
Building 30
1725 Van Patton Drive
Wright-Patterson AFB, OH 45433
(513)656-3104

DCMC Detroit
Building 231
Warren, MI 48397-5000
(810) 574-4474

DCMC Grand Rapids
Riverview Center Building
678 Front Street, NW
Grand Rapids, MI 49504-5352
(616) 456-2620

DCMC Hartford

DCMC Indianapolis

130 Darlin Street
E. Hartford, CT 06108-
3234
(860) 291-7705/7715

8899 E. 56th Street
Indianapolis, IN 46249-5701
(317) 510-2015/2088

DCMC Long Island
605 Stewart Avenue
Garden City, Long Island,
NY 11530-4761
(516) 228-5722

DCMC New York
Ft. Wadesworth
207 New York Avenue
Staten Island, NY 10305-5013
(718) 390-1016/1017

DCMC Orlando
3555 Maguire Boulevard
Orlando, FL 32803-3726
(407) 228-5113/5260

DCMC Philadelphia
2800 South 20th Street
P. O. Box 7699
Philadelphia, PA 19145
(215) 737-5818/3560

DCMC Pittsburgh
1612 William Moorhead
Federal Bldg.
1000 Liberty Avenue
Pittsburgh, PA 15222-
4190
(412) 395-5926

DCMC Reading
201 Penn St., Suite 201
Reading, PA 19601-4054
(610) 320-5012

DCMC Springfield
Building 1, ARDEC
Picatinny, NJ 07806-5000
(201) 724-8204

DCMC Stratford
550 Main Street
Stratford, CT 06497-7574
(203) 385-4416

DCMC Syracuse
615 Erie Boulevard, West
Syracuse, NY 13204-2408
(315) 448-7897/7809

WEST

DCMD West
222 N. Sepulveda Boulevard
El Segundo, CA 90245-4320
(310) 335-
3260/3262/3265/3285
Toll Free: (800) 624-7372

DCMC Dallas
1200 Main Street
Dallas, TX 75202-4399
(214)670-9205
Toll Free: (800)255-8574,
x1205
CA Only: (800) 233-6521

DCMC Chicago
O'Hare International Airport

DCMC Denver
Orchard Place 2, Suite 200

PO Box 66911 5975
(773)825-6021/6866
Toll Free: (800) 637-3848

Greenwood Plaza Blvd.
Englewood, CO 80110-4715
(303) 843-4300
Toll Free: (800)772-8975

DCMC Phoenix
Two Renaissance Square
40 N. Central Ave., Suite 400
Phoenix, AZ 85004
(602) 594-7809, x231

DCMC San Antonio
615 E. Houston Street
P. O. Box 1040
San Antonio, TX 78294-1040
(210) 472-4650

DCMC San Diego
7675 Dagget St., Suite 100
San Diego, CA 92111-2241
(619) 637-4922

DCMC San Francisco
1265 Borregas Avenue
Sunnyvale, CA 94089
(408) 541-7042

DCMC Santa Ana
34 Civic Center Plaza
P. O. Box C-12700
Santa Ana, CA 92712-2700
(714) 836-2700

DCMC Seattle
3009 112th Avenue, N.E.
Suite 200
Bellevue, WA 98004-8019
(425) 889-7317/7318

DCMC St. Louis
1222 Spruce Street
St. Louis, MO 63103-2811
(314) 331-5476
Toll Free: (800) 325-3419

DCMC Twin Cities
3001 Metro Dr., Suite 200
Bloomington, MN 55425-1573
(612) 814-4103

DCMC Van Nuys
6230 Van Nuys Boulevard
Van Nuys, CA 91401-2713
(818) 756-4444, x201

DCMC Wichita
217 West Third Street,
North
Suite 6000
Wichita, KS 67202-1212
(316) 299-7218

DEFENSE CONTRACT MANAGEMENT DISTRICT INTERNATIONAL

DCMC Puerto Rico
209 Chapel Drive
Navy Security Group Activity
Sabana Seca, PR 00952
(787) 795-3202
Defense Distribution Region West
ATTN: ASCW-PSS
Building S-4, Sharpe Site

Lathrop, CA 95331-5108
(209) 982-2435

Defense Distribution Region East
ATTN: ASCE-PA
New Cumberland, PA 17070
(717) 770-7107

SMALL BUSINESS ADMINISTRATION - PROCUREMENT ASSISTANCE OFFICES

These Procurement Assistance Offices of the SBA work closely with the principal buying agencies of the Federal Government. They can help you find the offices which are most likely to buy your products or services. They investigate the merits of appeals from unfavorable determinations of responsibility by contracting officers , and issue certificates of competency where warranted.

Area I

Small Business
Administration
10 Causeway Street,
Room 265
Boston, MA 02222-0193
(617) 565-5622

Connecticut, Maine,
Massachusetts, New
Hampshire, RI, Vermont

Small Business
Administration
26 Federal Plaza, Room
3108
New York, NY 10278
(212) 264-1452

New Jersey, New York, Puerto
Rico, Virgin Islands

Area II

Small Business
Administration
Allendale Square - Suite
201
475 Allendale Road
King of Prussia, PA 19406
(610) 962-3706

District of Columbia,
Delaware, Maryland,
Pennsylvania, Virginia, West
Virginia

Area III

Small Business

Alabama, Florida, Georgia,

Administration
1720 Peachtree Street,
N.W.,
Suite 496
Atlanta, GA 30309-2482
(404) 347-4483

Kentucky, Mississippi, North
Carolina, South Carolina,
Tennessee

Area VI

Small Business
Administration
Office of Government
Contracting
500 West Madison St.,
Suite 1250
Chicago, IL 60661-2511
(312) 353-7381

Illinois, Indiana, Michigan,
Minnesota, Ohio, Wisconsin

Small Business
Administration
Office of Government
Contracting
323 West 8th Street, Suite
501
Kansas City, MO 64105
(816) 374-6815

Iowa, Kansas,
Missouri,Nebraska

Area V

Small Business
Administration
4300 Amon Carter
Boulevard,
Suite 116
Ft. Worth, TX 76155
(817)334-5902

Arkansas, Louisiana, New
Mexico, Oklahoma, Texas

Small Business
Administration
Office of Government
Contracting
721 19th Street, Suite 447
Denver, CO 80202-2599
(303-844-0510

Colorado, Montana, North
Dakota, South Dakota, Utah,
Wyoming

Area VI

Small Business Administration 455 Market Street, Suite 2200 San Francisco, CA 94105 (415) 744-8429	Arizona, California, Guam, Hawaii, Nevada
Small Business Administration 1200 Sixth Avenue, Suite 1805 Seattle, WA 98101-1128 (206) 553-6850	Alaska, Idaho, Oregon, Washington

GENERAL SERVICES ADMINISTRATION BUSINESS SERVICE CENTERS

These Centers of the GSA are the "front doors" to contracting with GSA. Each center is staffed with Business Specialists who can provide you with information or assistance.

General Services Administration 7th & D Streets, SW Washington, DC 20407 (202) 708-5804	National Capital Region, District of Columbia, nearby Maryland and Virginia

Region I

General Services Administration O'Neill Federal Office Building 10 Causeway Street Boston, MA 02222 (617) 565-8100	Connecticut, Maine, Massachusetts, New Hampshire, Rhode Island Vermont

Region II

General Services Administration Jacob K. Javits Building Business Service Center 26 Federal Plaza	New Jersey, New York, Puerto Rico, Virgin Islands

New York, NY 10278
(212) 264-1234

Region III

General Services Administration
Wanamaker Building
100 Penn Square East
Philadelphia, PA 19107
(215) 656-5525

Delaware, Maryland, Pennsylvania, West Virginia, Virginia

Region IV

General Services Administration
Business Service Center
401 West Peachtree Street, Suite 2900
Atlanta, GA 30365-2550
(404) 331-5103

Alabama, Florida, Georgia, Kentucky, Mississippi, North Carolina, South Carolina, Tennessee

Region V

General Services Administration
230 South Dearborn Street
Chicago, IL 60604
(312) 353-5383

Illinois, Indiana, Michigan, Minnesota, Ohio, Wisconsin

Region VI

General Services Administration
Office of Business & Support Services
1500 East Bannister Road
Kansas City, MO 64131-3088
(816) 926-7203

Iowa, Kansas, Missouri, Nebraska

Region VII

General Services Administration

Arkansas, Louisiana, New Mexico, Oklahoma, Texas

819 Taylor Street, Room 11A05
Fort Worth, TX 76102
(817) 978-3284

Region VIII

General Services Administration
Denver Federal Center, Building 41
Business Service Center
P. O. Box 25006, Room 2530
Denver, CO 80225-0506
(303) 236-7408

North Dakota, Colorado, South Dakota, Utah, Wyoming, Montana

Region IX

General Services Administration
450 Goldgate Avenue, Room 0405
San Francisco, CA 94102
(415) 522-2700

Northern California, Hawaii, and all of Nevada except Clark County

General Services Administration
300 North Los Angeles Street
Room 3259
Los Angeles, CA 90012-2000
(213) 894-3210

Los Angeles, Southern California, Arizona, Neveda, Clark County

Region X

General Services Administration
15th & C Street, SW
Room 9AB-10
Auburn, WA 98001
(253) 931-7956

Appendix A:

ADDITIONAL SOURCES OF INFORMATION

REGULATIONS

"Federal Acquisition Regulation"

Available on a subscription basis from the Superintendent of Documents, U.S. Government Printing Office, Washington, D.C. 20402.

"DoD Federal Acquisition Regulation Supplement"

Available on a subscription basis from the Superintendent of Documents, U.S. Government Printing Office, Washington, D.C. 20402.

These regulations can also be found on the internet at: http://www.acq.osd.mil/.

MARKETING INFORMATION

"Commerce Business Daily (CBD)"

A daily list of proposed Federal Government procurements estimated to exceed $25,000. Also contains lists of subcontracting leads, sales of surplus property, and foreign business opportunities. Subscriptions may be made through the Superintendent of Documents, U.S. Government Printing Office, Washington, D.C. 20402. You can also access the CBDNet at http://cbdnet.gpo.gov . CBDNet is the official Free online listing of Government contracting opportunities which are published in the CBD.

"U.S. Government Purchasing and Sales Directory"

Provides a listing of products and services bought by all Federal agencies, keyed to the purchasing offices that buy them. Also provides information on Government sales of surplus property. Available from the Superintendent of Documents, U.S. Government Printing Office, Washington, D.C. 20402. Stock No. 045-000-00272-1, Cost $24.00 "Subcontracting Opportunities with DoD Major Prime Contractors"

Provides company name and address, product or service line, and name and telephone number of company's small business liaison officer for DoD prime contractors that have plans and goals (set forth in their prime contracts) for subcontracting with small business and small disadvantaged business concerns. Available from the Superintendent of Documents, U.S. Government Printing Office, Washington, D.C. 20402. The DoD reference number is 4205.1-D. This can also be found on the internet at: http://www.acq.osd.mil/.

"A Guide for Private Industry"

Tells how to obtain information regarding specifications and standards from the DoD Single Stock Point for Specifications and Standards. Available from the Naval Publications and Forms Center, 5801 Tabor Avenue, Philadelphia, PA. 19120.

AIDS FOR SMALL BUSINESSES

"Small Business Specialists"

On a nationwide basis, lists DoD specialists by name, location, and phone number. For sale by the Superintendent of Documents, U.S. Government Printing Office, Washington, D.C. 20402. The DoD reference number is DoD 4205.1-H. More information is available on the internet at: http://www.acq.osd.mil.

Procurement Marketing and Access Network (Pro-Net)

Pro-Net is an electronic source of procurement information – for and about small businesses. It is a search engine for contracting officers, a marketing tool for small firms and a "link" to procurement opportunities and important information. It is designed to be a "virtual" one-stop-procurement-shop.

Pro-Net is an Internet-based database of information on small, disadvantaged, 8(a) and women-owned businesses. It is free to federal and state government agencies as well as prime and other contractors seeking small business contractors, subcontractors and/or partnership opportunities.

Guidelines on how to register with Pro-Net is located at: http://www.sba.gov .

MANAGEMENT AIDS

Short papers providing specific guidance on various topics (available from nearest SBA office.)

"A Handbook for DoD and Small Business: Forging a Partnership Through EDI"

The purpose of this special report is to acquaint small business with the concepts of electronic data interchange (EDI) and how EDI will be used in the future by the Department of Defense to conduct business. The special report introduces the reader to EDI, discusses how and why EDI is used in business, and explains what is needed to start using EDI in a small business. Available for purchase from the National Technical Information Service, (703) 487-4650, order number is. ADA-261-373, and cost $27.00.

"Department of the Army's Electronic Capabilities"

The Army fully supports Electronic Commerce (EC) and its wide range of procuring government commodities electronically. Ninety-four percent (94%) of our contracting sites are Interim FACNET certified which allow small businesses to conduct transactions via Electronic Data Interchange (EDI). These type purchases are exclusively designated for small businesses procuring within the micro-purchase threshold ($2500 to $100K). http://procnet.pica.army.mil.

"Department of the Navy's Electronic Capabilities"

Marketing information is now available from the DoN Market Research Information Service on the World Wide Web (WWW). The database will help prospective contractors determine which supplies and services are being purchased at navy and Marine Corps contracting centers located throughout the United States. In addition to this marketing information, the DoN Long Range Acquisition Estimates is also on the WWW. The Internet address is http://www.abm.rda.hq.navy.mil/ .

"Department of the Air Force's Electronic Capabilities"

The Long Range Acquisition Estimate (LRAE) is a searchable database, which covers over 2,000 projected "Requests for Proposals", with buying activities, estimated dollar amounts, award dates, points of contact and other information potential suppliers need to formulate marketing strategies. Information on the LRAE is on Department of Air Force home page. The internet address is http://www.selltoairforce.org.

With this system, small businesses can identify all Air Force activities, with a description of what they buy, current contacts, addresses and telephone numbers. An E-mail capability between all users and counselors is available, as is an extensive electronic library for downloading reference and training materials. Real-time conferences are conducted with recognized experts on marketing specific activities and on areas of special interest.

For more information, contact the Department of Air Force, Small and Disadvantaged Business Office.

Appendix B:

SMALL AND DISADVANTAGED BUSINESS UTILIZATION OFFICES

Department of Agriculture
14th & Independence Ave., SW
Room 1323, South Bldg
Washington, DC 20250-9400
Telephone: (202) 720-7117
FAX: (202) 720-3001
www.usda.gov/

Department of the Treasury
1500 Penn. Ave., NW
Room 6100 Annex
Washington, DC 20220
Telephone: (202) 622-0530
FAX: (202) 622-2273
www.ustreas.gov/sba

Department of Commerce
14th & Constitution Ave., NW
Room 6411
Washington, DC 20230
Telephone: (202) 482-1472
FAX: (202) 482-0501
www.osec.doc.gov/osdbu

Environmental Protection Agency
401 M Street, SW, Code A-1230-C
Washington, DC 20460
Telephone: (703) 305-7777
FAX: (703) 305-6462

Corporation for National & Comm. Service
1100 Vermont Avenue, NW
Suite 2101
Washington, DC 20525
Telephone: (202) 606-5020
FAX: (202) 606-5126

Executive Office of the President
725 17th St., NW, Room 5001
Washington, DC 20503
Telephone: (202) 395-7669
FAX: (202) 395-1155

Agency for International Dev.
Ronald Reagan Bldg.
1300 Penn. Ave., NW
Telephone: (202) 712-1500
FAX: (202) 216-3056
www.info.usaid.gov

Department of Education
600 Independence Ave., SW
Room 3120, ROB 3
Washington, DC 20202-0521
Telephone: (202) 708-9820
FAX: (202) 401-6477
www.ed.gov/

General Services Administration
18th & F St., NW, Room 6029
Washington, DC 20405
Telephone: (202) 501-1021
FAX: (202) 208-5938
www.gsa.gov/

Civic Transportation Board
12th & Constitution Ave., NW
Room 3148
Washington, DC 20423
Telephone: (202) 565-1674/1596

Export-Import Bank of the U.S.
811 Vermont Ave., NW, Room 1017
Washington, DC 20571
Telephone: (202) 565-3338
FAX: (202) 565-3528

Federal Trade Commission
6th & Penn. Ave., NW
Room H-700
Washington, DC 20580
Telephone: (202) 326-2258
FAX: (202) 326-3529
www.ftc.gov

Nuclear Regulatory Commission
Mail Stop T2 F-18
Washington, DC 20555
Telephone: (301) 415-7380
FAX: (301) 415-5953

Department of Energy
1000 Independence Ave., SW Room 5810
Washington, DC 20585
Telephone: (202) 586-8383
FAX: (202) 586-3075
www.hr.doe.gov/

Depart. Of Health & Human Service
200 Independence Ave., SW
Room 517-D
Washington, DC 20201
Telephone: (202) 690-7300
FAX: (202) 690-8772

Depart. Of Housing & Urban Dev.
451 7th Street, SW, Room 3130
Washington, DC 20410
Telephone: (202) 708-1428
FAX: (202) 708-7642
www.hud.gov

Department of the Interior
18th & C ST., NW, Room 2727
Washington, DC 20240
Telephone: (202) 208-3493
FAX: (202) 208-5048
www.doi.gov/

Department of Justice
1331 Penn. Ave., NW
National Place Bldg., Room 1010
Washington, DC 20530
Telephone: (202) 616-0521
FAX: (202) 616-1717
www.usdoj.gov/

Office of Personnel

Department of Labor

124

Management
1900 E St., NW, Room 5542
Washington, DC 20415
Telephone: (202) 606-2180
FAX: (202) 219-0167

National Aeronautics &
Space Administration
Headquarters Code K, Room
9K 70
300 E. Street, SW
Washington, DC 20546
Telephone: (202) 358-2088
FAX: (202) 358-3261
www.nasa.gov/

National Science Foundation
4201 Wilson Blvd.
Arlington, VA 22230
Telephone: (703) 306-1390
FAX: (703) 306-0337
www.eng.nsf.gov/

Department of State
Room 633 (SA-6)
Washington, DC 20522-0602
Telephone: (703) 875-6824
FAX: (703) 875-6825

Department of Transportation
400 7th St., SW, Room 9414
Washington, DC 20590
Telephone: (202) 366-1930
FAX: (202) 366-7228
http://osdbuweb.dot.gov

200 Constitution Ave, NW
Room C 2318
Washington, DC 20210
Telephone: (202) 219-9148
FAX: (202) 606-1464
www.dol.gov/

Department of Veterans
Affairs
810 Vermont Ave., NW
Washington, DC 20420
Telephone: (202) 565-8124
FAX: (202) 565-8156
www.va.gov

U.S. Postal Service
475 L'Enfant Plaza West,
SW
Room 3821
Washington, DC 20260-
5616
Telephone: (202) 268-6578
FAX: (202) 268-6573
www.usps.gov

R.R. Retirement Board
844 N. Rush St.
Chicago, IL 60611
Telephone: (312) 751-4565
FAX: (312) 751-4923
www.rrb.gov

Office of Federal
Procurement Policy
725 17th St., NW, Room
9013
Washington, DC 20503
Telephone: (202) 395-3302
FAX: (202) 395-5105
www.arnet.gov

Small Business Administration
409 3rd St., SW, Eight Floor
Washington, DC 20416
Telephone: (202) 205-7701
FAX: (202) 693- 7004
www.sba.gov

Federal Emergency Management Agency
500 C St., SW, Room 726
Washington, DC 20472
Telephone: (202) 646-3743
FAX: (202) 646-3846
www.fema.gov/

Smithsonian Institute
915 L'Enfant Plaza, SW
Washington, DC 20506
Telephone: (202) 287-3588
FAX: (202) 287-3492

Army Corps of Engineers
20 Massachusetts Ave., NW
Washington, DC 20314
Telephone: (202) 761-0725
FAX: (202) 761-4609

Procurement Technical Assistance Center Program
George Mason University
7960 Donegan Dr., Sudley North Blg. B
Manassas, VA 22110
FAX: 703-330-5458

U.S. Information Agency
Donahue Bldg., Room 1725
400 6th St., SW
Washington, DC 20547
Telephone: (202) 205-9662
FAX: (202)401-2410

Tennessee Valley Authority
1101 Market St.
EB2B
Chattanooga, TN 37402-2801
Telephone: (423) 751-7203
FAX: (423) 751-7613

Minority Business Dev. Agency
Department of Commerce
Room 5093
14th & Constitution Ave., NW
Washington, DC 20230
Telephone: (202) 482-1712
FAX: (202) 482-5117

Appendix C:

GLOSSARY OF DEFENSE ACRONYMS

A

Aa	Achieved Availability
AAA	Army Audit Agency
AAE	Army Acquisition Executive
AAN	Army After Next
ABCA	American-British-Canadian-Australian
AC	Active Component
ACAP	Army Cost Analysis Paper
ACAT	Acquisition Category
ACC	Air Combat Command
ACE	Acquisition Center of Excellence
ACI	Allocated Configuration Identification
ACMC	Assistant Commandant of the Marine Corps
ACNO	Assistant Chief of Naval Operations
ACO	Administrative Contracting Officer
ACS	Assistant Chief of Staff
ACS/I	Assistance Chief of Staff for Intelligence (AF)
ACSN	Advance Change Study Notice
ACTD	Advanced Concept Technology Demonstration
ACWP	Actual Cost of Work Performed
ADM	Acquisition Decision Memorandum
ADP	Automated Data Processing
ADPE	ADP Equipment
ADR	Alternate Dispute Resolution/Alternative Dispute Resolution
AECA	Arms Export Control Act (1976)
AFAE	Air Force Acquisition Executive
AFALC	Air Force Air Logistics Center
AFCAA	Air Force Cost Analysis Agency
AFFTC	Air Force Flight Test Center
AFI	Air Force Instruction
AFIT	Air Force Institute of Technology
AFMC	Air Force Materiel Command
AFOTEC	Air Force Operational Test and Evaluation Center
AFPD	Air Force Policy Directive
Ai	Inherent Availability
AI	Artificial intelligence
AIS	Automated Information System
ALC	Air Logistics Center (AF)
ALMC	Army Logistics Management College
ALO	Authorized Level of Organization (Army)

AMC	Army Materiel Command; Air Mobility Command
AMCOM	Aviation and Missile Command (Army)
AMP	Army Modernization Plan
AMSAA	Army Materiel Systems Analysis Agency
AMSDL	Acquisition Management Systems Data List
Ao	Operational Availability
AoA	Analysis of Alternatives (formerly called COEA)
AP	Acquisition Plan
AP/A/N/AF	Aircraft Procurement (Appropriations), Army/Navy/Air Force
APB	Acquisition Program Baseline
APL	Approved Parts List
APPN	Appropriation
APUC	Average Procurement Unit Cost (also see AUPC)
AQAP	Allied Quality Assurance Provision
AR	Army Regulation; Acquisition Reform
ARL	Army Research Laboratory
ASA(ALT)	Assistant Secretary of the Army (Acquisition, Logistics, and Technology)
ASARC	Army Systems Acquisition Review Council
ASBCA	Armed Services Board of Contract Appeals
ASC	Aeronautical Systems Center (AF)
ASD(C3I)	Asst Secty of Def (Command, Control, Communications, and Intelligence)
ASD(LA)	Assistant Secretary of Defense (Legislative Affairs)
ASF	Army Stock Fund
ASN (M&RA)	Assistant Secretary of the Navy (Manpower and Reserve Affairs)
ASN (RD&A)	Assistant Secretary of the Navy (Research, Development and Acquisition)
ASR	Alternative Systems Review; Acquisition Strategy Report (obsolete)
ATC	Air Training Command
ATD	Advanced Technology Development/Demonstration
ATE	Automatic Test Equipment
ATEC	Army Test and Evaluation Command (Army)
ATP	Acceptance Test Procedures
ATPS	Automated Test Planning System
AUPC	Average Unit Procurement Cost (also see APUC)
AWACS	Airborne Warning and Control System (AF)
AWE	Advanced Warfighting Experiment

B

B&P	Bid and Proposal
BA	Budget Authority; Budget Activity
BAA	Broad Agency Announcement
BAC	Budgeted Cost at Completion
BAFO	Best and Final Offer

BCE	Baseline Cost Estimate (Army)
BCM	Baseline Correlation Matrix (AF)
BCS	Baseline Comparative System
BCWP	Budgeted Cost of Work Performed
BCWS	Budgeted Cost of Work Scheduled
BES	Budget Estimate Submission
BFM	Business and Financial Manager
BIOS	Basic Input/Output System
BIT	Built-In Test; Binary Digit
BITE	Built-In Test Equipment
BLRIP	Beyond Low Rate Initial Production
BMD	Ballistic Missile Defense
BMDO	Ballistic Missile Defense Organization
BMO	Ballistic Missile Office (AF)
BOA	Basic Ordering Agreement
BOIP	Basis of Issue Plan (Army)
BPR	Business Process Reengineering
BRAC	Base Realignment and Closure
BRP	Basic Research Plan
BT	Builder's Trials (Ships)
BUR	Bottom-Up Review
BY	Budget Year; Base Year

C

C-V-P	Cost-Volume-Profit
C/SSR	Cost/Schedule Status Report
C2	Command and Control
C3I	Command, Control, Communications, and Intelligence
C4	Command, Control, Communications, and Computers
C4I	Command, Control, Communications, Computers and Intelligence
C4ISP	Command, Control, Communications, Computers and Intelligence Support Plan
C4ISR	Command, Control, Communications, Computers, Intelligence, Surveillance and Reconnaissance
C4ISR AF	Command, Control, Communications, Computers, Intelligence, Surveillance and Reconnaissance Architecture Framework
CAD	Computer Aided Design; Component Advanced Development work effort (part of the Concept & Technology Development phase)
CAE	Component Acquisition Executive; Computer Aided Engineering
CAIG	Cost Analysis Improvement Group (OSD)
CAIV	Cost as an Independent Variable
CALS	Continuous Acquisition Lifecycle Support
CAM	Computer Aided Manufacturing
CAO	Contract Administration Office
CAP	Contractor Acquired Property; Critical Acquisition Position

CAR	Command Assessment Review (AF); Configuration Audit Review
CARS	Consolidated Acquisition Reporting System
CARD	Cost Analysis Requirements Description
CAS	Cost Accounting Standard; Contract Administration Services
CASE	Computer Aided System Engineering; Computer Aided Software Engineering
CAST	Computer Aided Software Testing
CAT	Computer Aided Testing
CATM	Computer Aided Technical Management
CBD	Commerce Business Daily; Chemical Biological Defense
CBDCOM	Chemical-Biological Defense Command (Army)
CBO	Congressional Budget Office
CBR	Chemical, Biological, Radiological; Concurrent Budget Resolution
CBTDEV	Combat Developments (Army/Marine Corps)
CCA	Component Cost Analysis; Clinger-Cohen Act
CCB	Configuration Control Board
CCDR	Contractor Cost Data Reporting
CCN	Contract Change Notice; Configuration Change Notice
CCP	Contract Change Proposal
CDR	Critical Design Review
CDRL	Contract Data Requirements List
CE	Current Estimate; Concept Exploration work effort (part of the Concept and Technology Development phase)
CEAC	Cost and Economic Analysis Center (Army)
CECOM	Communications and Electronics Command (Army)
CEP	Circular Error Probable; Contract Estimating and Pricing; Concept Evaluation Program (Army)
CER	Cost Estimating Relationship
CETS	Contractor Engineering and Technical Services
CFE	Contractor Furnished Equipment
CFEN	Contractor Furnished Equipment Notice
CFM	Contractor Financial Management; Contractor Furnished Material
CFO	Chief Financial Officer
CFSR	Contract Funds Status Report
CG	Chairman's Guidance (JCS); Commanding General
CI	Configuration Item; Counterintelligence
CIC	Critical Intelligence Category
CICA	Competition in Contracting Act (1984)
CID	Commercial Item Description
CINC	Commander-in-Chief
CIO	Chief Information Officer
CIP	Component Improvement Program; Critical Intelligence Parameter
CITA	Commercial or Industrial-Type Activities
CITIS	Contractor Integrated Technical Information Service
CJCS	Chairman, Joint Chiefs of Staff
CLIN	Contract Line Item Number

CLS	Contractor Logistics Support
CM	Configuration Management; Contract Management
CMC	Commandant of the Marine Corps
CMIS	Configuration Management Information System
CMM	Capability Maturity Model
CMMI	Capability Maturity Model - Integrated
CMP	Configuration Management Plan
CAN	Center for Naval Analysis
CNAD	Conference of NATO Armaments Directors
CNO	Chief of Naval Operations
CO	Contracting Officer; Change Order; Commanding Officer
COBOL	Common Business Oriented Language
COC	Certificate of Competency; Certification of Compliance
COCO	Contractor Owned/Contractor Operated (Facilities)
COCOMO	Constructive Cost Model (for software)
COE	Common Operating Environment (aka DIICOE)
COEA	Cost and Operational Effectiveness Analysis (obsolete - see AoA)
COI	Critical Operational Issue
COMDT	Commandant
COMMINT	Communications Intelligence
COMOPTEVFOR	Commander, Operational Test and Evaluation Force (Navy)
COMPT	Comptroller
CONUS	Continental United States
COR/COTR	Contracting Officer's (Technical) Representative
COTS	Commercial Off-The-Shelf
CPA	Chairman's Program Assessment (JCS)
CPAF	Cost-Plus-Award Fee
CPAM	CNO Program Assessment Memorandum (Navy)
CPAR	Contractor Performance Assessment Report (AF)
CPC	Corrosion Prevention and Control
C/PD	Cost/Pricing Data
CPFF	Cost-Plus-Fixed Fee
CPI	Cost Performance Index; Consumer Price Index
CPIF	Cost-Plus-Incentive Fee
CPIPT	Cost Performance Integrated Product Team
CPM	Critical Path Method; Contractor Performance Measurement
CPO/CCPO	(Consolidated) Civilian Personnel Office
CPR	Cost Performance Report; Chairman's Program Recommendation
CPS	Competitive Prototyping Strategy
CPSR	Contractor Procurement/Purchasing System Review
CPU	Central Processing Unit
CR	Cost Reimbursement; Continuing Resolution; Change Request
CRA	Continuing Resolution Authority
CRAG	Contractor Risk Assessment Guide
CRD	Capstone Requirements Document
CRISD	Computer Resources Integrated Support Document

CRLCMP	Computer Resources Life Cycle Management Plan
CRWG	Computer Resource Working Group
CSA	Chief of Staff of the Army
CSAF	Chief of Staff of the Air Force
CSC	Computer Software Component
CSCI	Computer Software Configuration Item (aka SI)
CSOM	Computer Software Operator's Manual
CSS	Contractor Support Services
CSSR	Cost Schedule Status Report
CSU	Computer Software Unit
C&TD	Concept and Technology Development (phase of the life cycle)
CTEA	Cost and Training Effectiveness Analysis (Army)
CTEMP	Capstone Test and Evaluation Master Plan
CTP	Critical Technical Parameter
CWBS	Contract Work Breakdown Structure
CY	Calendar Year; Current Year

D

D&F	Determination and Findings
DA	Department of the Army; Developing Agency/Activity
DAB	Defense Acquisition Board
DAC	Defense Acquisition Circular; Designated Acquisition Commander (AF)
DAE	Defense Acquisition Executive
DAES	Defense Acquisition Executive Summary
DAF	Department of the Air Force
DARC	Defense Acquisition Regulatory Council
DARPA	Defense Advanced Research Projects Agency (formerly ARPA)
DASC	Department of the Army Systems Coordinator
DASD	Deputy Assistant Secretary of Defense
DAU	Defense Acquisition University
DAWIA	Defense Acquisition Workforce Improvement Act
DBDD	Data Base Design Document
DBOF	Defense Business Operations Fund (obsolete – see WCF)
DC/S (I&L)	Deputy Chief of Staff, Installations and Logistics (USMC)
DCAA	Defense Contract Audit Agency
DCAS	Defense Contract Administration Services
DCMA	Defense Contract Management Agency
DCMAO	Defense Contract Management Area Operations (obsolete)
DCMC	Defense Contract Management Command (obsolete - see DCMA)
DCMR	Defense Contract Management Regions
DCNO	Deputy Chief of Naval Operations
DCOR	Defense Committee on Research
DCS	Deputy Chief of Staff
DCSINT	Deputy Chief of Staff for Intelligence (Army and AF)
DCSLOG	Deputy Chief of Staff for Logistics (Army)

DCSOPS	Deputy Chief of Staff for Operations and Plans (Army)
DCSPER	Deputy Chief of Staff for Personnel (Army)
DDN	Defense Data Network
DDR&E	Director, Defense Research and Engineering (OSD)
DEM/VAL, D/V	Demonstration/Validation (budget activity)
DEPSECDEF	Deputy Secretary of Defense
DESC	Defense Electronic Supply Center
DESCOM	Depot System Command (Army)
DFARS	DoD FAR Supplement
DFAS	Defense Finance and Accounting Service
DIA	Defense Intelligence Agency
DIB	Defense Industrial Base
DII	Defense Information Infrastructure
DIICOE	Defense Information Infrastructure Common Operating Environment
DID	Data Item Description
DIPEC	Defense Industrial Plant Equipment Center
DISA	Defense Information Systems Agency
DISAM	Defense Institute of Security Assistance Management
DISN	Defense Information Systems Network
DLA	Defense Logistics Agency
D Level	Depot Level of Maintenance
DMA	Defense Mapping Agency (obsolete – see NIMA)
DML	Depot Maintenance Level
DMS	Defense Materials System
DoD	Department of Defense
DoDD	Department of Defense Directive
DoDI	Department of Defense Instruction
DODIC	Department of Defense Identification Code
DoDIG	Department of Defense Inspector General
DODIIS	Department of Defense Intelligence Information System
DoD-R	Department of Defense - Regulation
DoD-M	Department of Defense - Manual
DoDISS	Department of Defense Index of Specifications and Standards
DOE	Design of Experiments
DoE	Department of Energy
DON	Department of the Navy
DOT&E	Director, Operational Test and Evaluation (OSD)
DPA	Defense Production Act
DPESO	DoD Product Engineering Services Office
DPG	Defense Planning Guidance
DPM	Deputy Program Manager
DPML	Deputy Program Manager for Logistics
DPP	Defense Program Projection
DPRO	Defense Plant Representatives Office (obsolete - now DCMC (plant name))
DR	Decision Review (DoDI 5000.2)

DRB	Defense Resources Board
DRM	DAB Readiness Meeting
DRPM	Direct Reporting Program Manager(s)
DPP	Defense Program Projection
DPS	Decision Package Sets; Defense Priorities System
DR	Decision Review
DSAA	Defense Security Assistance Agency
DSAC	Defense Systems Affordability Council
DSB	Defense Science Board
DSMC	Defense Systems Management College
DSP	Defense Standardization Program
DSSP	Defense Standardization and Specification Program
DS&TS	Director, Strategic and Tactical Systems
DT	Developmental Test; Developmental Testing
DTAP	Defense Technology Area Plan
DTC	Design-to-Cost
DT&E	Developmental Test and Evaluation
DTIC	Defense Technical Information Center
DTLCC	Design to Life Cycle Cost
DTLOMS	Doctrine, Training, Leader Development, Organization, Materiel, and Soldier (Army)
DTO	Defense Technology Objective
DT/OT	Developmental Testing/Operational Testing (combined effort)
DTRA	Defense Threat Reduction Agency
DTUPC	Design-to-Unit Production Cost
DUSD(AR)	Deputy Under Secretary of Defense (Acquisition Reform)

E

E3	Electromagnetic Environmental Effects
EA	Evolutionary Acquisition; Environmental Assessment
EAC	Estimated Cost at Completion
EAPROM	Electronically Alterable Programmable Read-Only Memory
ECAC	Electromagnetic Compatibility Analysis Center
ECCM	Electronic Counter-Countermeasures
EC/EDI	Electronic Commerce/Electronic Data Interchange
ECM	Electronic Countermeasures
ECN	Engineering Change Notice
ECP	Engineering Change Proposal
EDM	Engineering Development Model
EDP/E	Electronic Data Processing/Equipment
EEPROM	Electronically Erasable Programmable Read-Only Memory
EIR	Equipment Improvement Recommendation (Army)
EIS	Environmental Impact Statement
ELINT	Electronic Intelligence
EMC	Electromagnetic Compatibility

EMD	Engineering and Manufacturing Development (phase of the life cycle)
EMI	Electromagnetic Interference
EMP	Electromagnetic Pulse
EO	Executive Order
EOA	Early Operational Assessment
EOQ	Economic Ordering Quantity
EP	Electronic Protect
EPA	Environmental Protection Agency, Economic Price Adjustment
EPROM	Erasable Programmable Read-Only Memory
ESC	Electronics Systems Center (AF)
ESH	Environmental, Safety and Health
ESOH	Environment, Safety and Occupational Health
ETR	Estimated Time to Repair
EVM	Earned Value Management
EVMS	Earned Value Management Standard
EW	Electronic Warfare

F

F3/FFF	Form-Fit-Function
F3I	Form-Fit-Function Interface
FA/A	Functional Analysis/Allocation
FAC	Federal Acquisition Circular
FACNET	Federal Acquisition Computer Network
FAR	Federal Acquisition Regulation
FARA	Federal Acquisition Reform Act of 1996
FASA	Federal Acquisition Streamlining Act of 1994
FAT	First Article Testing; Factory Acceptance Test
FC	Fixed Cost
FCA	Functional Configuration Audit
FCRC	Federal Contract Research Center
FCT	Foreign Comparative Testing
FDR	Final/Formal Design Review
FDTE	Force Development Testing and Experimentation (Army)
FFP	Firm Fixed Price
FFRDC	Federally Funded R&D Center
FFW	Failure-Free Warranty
FIT	Fault Isolation Tree
FLOT	Forward Line of Troops; Flotilla
FM	Financial Management
FMEA	Failure Mode and Effects Analysis
FMECA	Failure Mode and Effects Criticality Analysis
FMF	Fleet Marine Force
FMP	Fleet Modernization Plan (Navy)
FMS	Foreign Military Sales; Flexible Machining System
FOC	Full Operational Capability

FOIA	Freedom of Information Act
FOS	Family of Systems
FONSI	Finding of No Significant Impact
FOT&E	Follow-on Operational Test and Evaluation
FPAF	Fixed Price Award Fee
FPBD	Functional Plan Block Diagram
FPDS	Federal Procurement Data System
FPEPA	Fixed Price with Economic Price Adjustment
FPIF	Fixed Price Incentive (Firm)
FPIS	Fixed Price Incentive (Successive Target)
FQR	Functional/Formal Qualification Review
FRACAS	Failure Reporting, Analysis and Corrective Action System
FRP	Full Rate Production
FRP&D	Full Rate Production and Deployment work effort (part of the Production and Deployment Phase)
FRPDR	Full Rate Production Decision Review
FS	Flexible Sustainment
FSA	Functional Systems Audit
FSCM	Federal Supply Code for Manufacturers
FSG	Federal Stock Group
FSM	Firmware Support Manual
FSN	Federal Stock Number
FSS	Federal Supply Schedule
FUE	First Unit Equipped
FY	Fiscal Year
FYDP	Future Years Defense Program

G

G&A	General and Administrative
GAO	General Accounting Office
GAT	Government Acceptance Test
GBL	Government Bill of Lading
GDP	Gross Domestic Product
GFAE	Government Furnished Aeronautical Equipment
GFE	Government Furnished Equipment
GFF	Government Furnished Facilities
GFI	Government Furnished Information
GFM	Government Furnished Material
GFP	Government Furnished Property
GFS	Government Furnished Software
GIDEP	Government Industry Data Exchange Program
GIG	Global Information Grid
GNP	Gross National Product
GOCO	Government-Owned, Contractor-Operated (Facility)
GOGO	Government-Owned, Government-Operated (Facility)

GPETE	General Purpose Electronic Test Equipment
GPRA	Government Performance and Results Act
GPPC	Government Property in the Possession of Contractors
GSA	General Services Administration
GSBCA	General Services Board of Contract Appeals
GSE	Ground Support Equipment

H

H/W or HW	Hardware
HAC	House Appropriations Committee
HARDMAN	Manpower Planning for Hardware (Navy/USMC)
HASC	House Armed Services Committee
HBC	House Budget Committee
HCA	Head of Contracting Agency /Activity
HCI	Human-Computer Interface
HERO	Hazards of Electromagnetic Radiation to Ordnance
HFE	Human Factors Engineering
HOL	Higher Order Language
HQ	Headquarters
HQDA	Headquarters, Department of the Army
HQMC	Headquarters, Marine Corps
HSC	Human Systems Center (AF)
HIS	Human Systems Integration
HTI	Horizontal Technology Integration (Army)
HTML	HyperText Markup Language
HWCI	Hardware Configuration Item
HWIL	Hardware-in-the-Loop

I

I&L	Installations and Logistics
IA	Information Assurance
IBR	Integrated Baseline Review
ICA	Independent Cost Analysis
ICAF	Industrial College of the Armed Forces
ICD	Interface Control Drawing (or Document)
ICE	Independent Cost Estimate
ICEP	Information Certification Evaluation Plan
ICG	Interactive Computerized Graphic
ICP	Inventory Control Point
ICT	Integrated Concept Team (Army)
ICWG	Interface Control Working Group
IDA	Institute for Defense Analysis
IDD	Interface Design Document
IDE	Integrated Digital Environment

IE	Industrial Engineer
IER	Information Exchange Requirement
IES	Industrial Engineering Standard
IF	Industrial Fund
IFB	Invitation for Bid
IG	Inspector General
IGCE	Independent Government Cost Estimate
IIPT	Integrating IPT
I LEVEL	Intermediate Level of Maintenance
ILS OSD	Integrated Logistics Support (Army, Navy, & Air Force; replaced at
	level by the term "acquisition logistics")
ILSMT	ILS Management Team
IM	Item Manager
IML	Intermediate Maintenance Level
INF	Intermediate-Range Nuclear Forces
INFOSEC	Information Security
IOC	Initial Operational Capability; Industrial Operations Command (Army)
IOT&E	Initial Operational Test and Evaluation
IPCE	Independent Parametric Cost Estimate
IPD	Integrated Product Development
IPE	Industrial Plant Equipment
IPF	Initial Production Facilities
IPP	Industrial Preparedness Planning
IPPD	Integrated Product and Process Development
IPR Review;	Interim Progress Review (DoDI 5000.2); also In-Progress/Process
	Interim Program Review
IPT	Integrated Product Team
IR&D	Independent Research and Development
IRS	Interface Requirement Specification
ISA	International Security Affairs (OSD); International Standardization Agreement; Instruction Set Architecture
ISP	Integrated Support Plan; Internet Service Provider
IT	Information Technology
ITA	Integrated Technology Architecture
ITMRA	Information Technology Management Reform Act of 1996
IT OIPT	Information Technology Overarching Integrated Product Team
ITOPS	International Test Operations Procedures
ITP	Integrated Test Plan
ITS	Information Technology System
IV&V	Independent Verification and Validation
IW	Information Warfare
IWSM	Integrated Weapon System Management (AF)

J

J&A	Justification and Approval
JAMAC	Joint Aeronautical Materials Activity
JCALS	Joint Computer-Aided Acquisition and Logistics Support
JCS	Joint Chiefs of Staff
JEDMICS	Joint Engineering Data Management Information Control System
JIEO	Joint Interoperability and Engineering Organization
JIT	Just-in-Time
JITC	Joint Interoperability Test Command
JLC	Joint Logistics Commanders
JMNA	Joint Military Net Assessment (JCS/OSD)
JOA	Joint Operating Agreement; Joint Operational Architecture
JOP	Joint Operating Procedures
JPD	Joint Planning Document
JPO	Joint Program Office
JROC	Joint Requirements Oversight Council
JRB	Joint Requirements Board
JRP	Joint Requirements Panel
JSCP	Joint Strategic Capabilities Plan
JSPS	Joint Strategic Planning System
JSR	Joint Strategy Review (JCS)
JT&E	Joint Test and Evaluation
JTA	Joint Technical Architecture
JV 2020	Joint Vision (for the year) 2020
JWCA	Joint Warfare Capability Assessment
JWCO	Joint Warfare Capability Objective
JWE	Joint Warfighting Experiment
JWG	Joint Working Group
JWSTP	Joint Warfighting Science and Technology Plan

K

K	Contract
KPP	Key Performance Parameter
KO	Contracting Officer (Also CO)
KR/Kr/KTR/Ktr	Contractor

L

LL	Legislative Liaison/Long Lead
LA	Legislative Affairs; Legislative Assistant (Congress)
LAN	Local Area Network
LBTS	Land Based Test Site
LCC	Life Cycle Cost
LCCE	Life Cycle Cost Estimate

LCM	Life Cycle Management
LCSS	Life Cycle Software Support
LEM	Logistic Element Manager
LFP	Logistics Funding Profile
LFT&E	Live Fire Test and Evaluation
LISI	Levels of Information System Interoperability
LLT	Long Lead-Time (material and/or funding)
LM	Logistics Management
LMI	Logistics Management Institute; Logistics Management Information
LOA	Letter of Offer and Acceptance; Letter of Authorization
LOB	Line of Balance
LOC	Line of Code
LOE	Level of Effort; Letter of Evaluation (AF)
LOG	Logistics
LOGCAP	Logistics Command Assessment of Projects
LOGO	Limitation of Government Obligation
LOI	Letter of Instruction; Letter of Intent
LOR/A	Level of Repair/Analysis
LP	Limited Procurement
LRE	Latest Revised Estimate
LRG	Logistics Review Group (Navy)
LRIP	Low Rate Initial Production
LRP	Low Rate Production
LRRDAP	Long Range Research Development and Acquisition Plan (Army)
LRU	Line Replaceable Unit
LS	Logistic Support
LSA	Logistic Support Analysis (obsolete)
LSAR	Logistic Support Analysis Record (obsolete)
LSI	Large Scale Integration

M

M&S	Modeling and Simulation
MAA	Mission Area Analysis
MAAG	Military Assistance Advisory Group
MACOM	Major Command (Army)
MAGTF	Marine Air-Ground Task Force
MAIS	Major Automated Information System
MAISRC	Major Automated Information System Review Council (obsolete – see IT OIPT)
MAJCOM	Major Command (AF)
MANPRINT	Manpower and Personnel Integration (Army)
MANTECH/MT	Manufacturing Technology
MAOPR	Minimum Acceptable Operational Performance Requirement
MAR	Management Assessment Review; Monthly Activity Report
MARCORMATCOM	Marine Corps Materiel Command

MARCORSYSCOM	Marine Corps Systems Command
MATCOM	Materiel Command
MATDEV	Materiel Developer (Army)
MATE	Modular Automatic Test Equipment
MC/A/N/AF/MC	Military Construction (MILCON) (Appropriation), Army/Navy/AirForce/USMC
MCCDC	Marine Corps Combat Development Command
MCCR	Mission Critical Computer Resources
MCCS	Mission Critical Computer System
MCEB	Military Communications-Electronics Board
MCOTEA	Marine Corps Operational Test and Evaluation Activity
MCP	Mission Coordinating Paper; Military Construction Plan
MDA	Milestone Decision Authority
MDAP	Major Defense Acquisition Program
MDT	Mean Down Time
MFHBF	Mean Flight Hours Between Failure
MFP	Materiel Fielding Plan (Army); Major Force Program
MILCON	Military Construction (Appropriation)
MILDEP	Military Deputy
MILPERS	Military Personnel (Appropriation)
MILSCAP	Military Standard Contract Administration Procedure
MILSPEC	Military Specification
MILSTAMP	Military Standard Transportation and Movement Procedures
MILSTD	Military Standard
MILSTEP	Military Supply and Transportation Evaluation Procedures
MILSTRAP	Military Standard Transaction Reporting and Accounting Procedures
MILSTRIP	Military Standard Requisitioning and Issue Procedures
MIP/A/N/AF	Missile Procurement (Appropriation), Army/Navy/Air Force
MIPR	Military Interdepartmental Purchase Request
MIPS	Modified Integrated Program Summary (Army)
MIS	Management Information System
MLA	Military Liaison Assistant (Congress)
MLDT	Mean Logistics Delay Time
MMT	Manufacturing Methods Technology
MNA	Mission Needs Analysis
MND	Mission Need Determination
MNS	Mission Need Statement
MOA	Memorandum of Agreement
MOD	Modification; Ministry of Defense (Allied)
MOE	Measure of Effectiveness
MOP	Measure of Performance
MOS	Measure of Suitability
MOU	Memorandum of Understanding
MP/A/N/AF/M	Military Personnel (Appropriation), Army/Navy/Air Force/USMC
MPT	Manpower, Personnel and Training

MROC	Marine Requirements Oversight Council
MS or M/S	Milestone
MSC	Major Subordinate Command; Military Sealift Command
MSD	Material Support Date
MT/MANTECH	Manufacturing Technology
MTBF	Mean Time Between Failures
MTBMA	Mean Time Between Maintenance Actions
MTTR	Mean Time To Repair
MTW	Major Theater War
MYP	Multiyear Procurement

N

NAC	North Atlantic Council; Naval Avionics Center
NAE	Navy Acquisition Executive
NAPR	NATO Armaments Planning Review
NASA	National Aeronautics and Space Administration
NATO	North Atlantic Treaty Organization
NAVAIR	Naval Air Systems Command
NAVFAC	Naval Facilities Engineering Command
NAVSEA	Naval Sea Systems Command
NAVSUP	Naval Supply Systems Command
NBC	Nuclear, Biological, Chemical
NBCC	Nuclear, Biological, and Chemical Contamination
NCA	National Command Authority
NDI	Nondevelopmental Item
NDP	National Defense Panel
NDU	National Defense University
NEPA	National Environmental Policy Act
NIE	National Intelligence Estimate
NIGA	Nuclear Indirect Gamma Activity
NIMA	National Imagery and Mapping Agency
NMS	National Military Strategy
NRO	National Reconnaissance Office
NROC	Navy Requirements Oversight Council
NSA	National Security Agency
NSC	National Security Council
NSCCA	Nuclear Safety Cross-Check Analysis
NSF	Navy Stock Fund
NSS	National Security System/National Security Strategy
NTIS	National Technical Information Service (Department of Commerce)
NTP	Navy Training Plan
NWC	National War College; Navy War College; Nuclear Weapons Council; Nuclear Weapons Center
NWSC	Naval Weapons Support Center

O

O&M	Operation and Maintenance
O&S	Operations and Support
OA	Obligation Authority; Operational Assessment
OB	Operating Budget
OBE	Overcome By Events
OCD	Operational Concept Document (AF)
OCLL	Office, Chief of Legislative Liaison (Army)
OCSA	Office of the Chief of Staff, U.S. Army
OFPP	Office of Federal Procurement Policy (OMB)
OGC	Office of the General Counsel
OIPT	Overarching Integrated Product Team
OJT	On-the-Job Training
OLA	Office of Legislative Affairs (Navy)
OM/A/N/AF/MC	Operation and Maintenance (Appropriation), Army/Navy/AirForce/USMC
OMB	Office of Management and Budget
OMS/MP	Operational Mode Summary/Mission Profile
ONR	Office of Naval Research
OP/A/N/AF	Other Procurement (Appropriation), Army/Navy/Air Force
OPEVAL	Operational Evaluation (Navy)
OPM	Office of Personnel Management
OPNAV	Office of the Chief of Naval Operations
OPNAVINST	OPNAV Instruction (Navy)
OPR	Office of Primary Responsibility
OPSEC	Operations Security
OPTEVFOR	Operational Test and Evaluation Force (Navy)
ORD	Operational Requirements Document
OR/SA	Operations Research/Systems Analysis
OS	Operational Suitability; Open Systems
O&S	Operations and Support (phase of the life cycle)
OSA	Open Systems Architecture
OSD	Office of the Secretary of Defense
OSE	Open Systems Environment
OSIA	On-Site Inspection Agency
OT	Operational Testing
OT&E	Operational Test and Evaluation
OTA	Operational Test Agency
OTP	Operational Test Plan
OUSD(AT&L)	Office of the Under Secretary of Defense (Acquisition, Technology and Logistics)

P

P&A	Price and Availability

P&L	Profit and Loss
P&T	Personnel and Training
P3I	Preplanned Product Improvement
PA	Program Authorization (AF); Product Assurance
PA&E	Program Analysis and Evaluation
PAPS	Periodic Armaments Planning System (NATO)
PAT	Process Action Team
PAT&E	Production Acceptance Test and Evaluation
PAUC	Program Acquisition Unit Cost
PB	President's Budget
PBBE	Performance Based Business Environment (AF)
PBC	Performance Based Contracting
PBD	Program Budget Decision
PBWS	Performance (Based) Work Statement
PCA	Physical Configuration Audit
P-CMM	Personnel Capability Maturity Model
PCO	Procuring Contracting Officer
PCR	Program Change Request; Procurement Center Representative
PD	Program Director (AF)
P&D	Production and Deployment (phase of the life cycle)
PDM	Program Decision Memorandum (OSD); Program Decision Meeting (Navy, Marine Corps)
PDP	Program Development Plan
PDR	Preliminary Design Review
PDRR	Program Definition and Risk Reduction (obsolete)
PDSS	Post Deployment Software Support
PE	Planning Estimate; Program Element; Procurement Executive
PEM	Program Element Monitor (AF)
PEO	Program Executive Officer
PEP	Producibility Engineering and Planning
PERT	Program Evaluation Review Technique
PESO	Product Engineering Services Office
PESHE	Programmatic ESOH Evaluation
PF/DOS	Production, Fielding/Deployment, and Operational Support (of the life cycle)
PHST	Packaging, Handling, Storage, and Transportation
PI	Product Improvement
PIP	Product Improvement Proposal/Program
PIPT	Program-Level Integrated Product Team
Pk	Probability of Kill
PL	Public Law
PM	Program Manager; Project Manager; Product Manager
PMB	Performance Measurement Baseline
PMD	Program Management Document; Program Management Directive (AF)
PMJEG	Performance Measurement Joint Executive Group
PMO	Program Management Office

PMP	Program Management Plan
PMR	Program Management Review
POA&M	Plan of Actions and Milestones
POC	Point of Contact
POE	Program Office Estimate
POL	Petroleum, Oil and Lubricants
POM	Program Objectives Memorandum
POMCUS	Prepositioned Overseas Materiel Configured to Unit Sets
POP	Proof of Principle (Army)
PPBES	Planning, Programming, Budgeting, and Execution System (Army)
PPBS	Planning, Programming, and Budgeting System (DoD)
PPSS	Post Production Software Support
PPL	Provisioning Parts List
PPP	Program Protection Plan
PPS	Postproduction Support
PPSP	Postproduction Support Plan
PQT	Production Qualification Testing
PR	Procurement Request; Purchase Request
PRA	Paper Reduction Act
PRAT	Production Reliability Acceptance Test
PRG	Program Review Group
PROD	Production
PROM	Programmable Read-Only Memory
PRR	Production Readiness Review
PSA	Principal Staff Assistant
PSE	Peculiar Support Equipment
PSM	Professional Staff Member (Congress); Practical Software Measurement (OSD)
PTD	Provisioning Technical Documentation
PTTI	Precise Time and Time Interval
PWBS	Program Work Breakdown Structure
PWRMS	Prepositioned War Reserve Materiel Stocks
PY	Prior Year

Q

QA	Quality Assurance
QAR	Quality Assurance Representative
QBL	Qualified Bidders List
QC	Quality Control
QCR	Qualitative Construction Requirement
QDR	Quadrennial Defense Review
QFD	Quality Function Deployment
QPL	Qualified Products List
QQPRI	Qualitative and Quantitative Personnel Requirement Information (Army)
QRC	Quick Reaction Capability

R

R&D	Research and Development
R&M	Reliability and Maintainability
RAD	Request for Authority to Develop (an international agreement)
RAM	Random Access Memory; Reliability, Availability and Maintainability
RAP	Resource Allocation Process
RBA	Revolution in Business Affairs
RBL	Reliability Based Logistics
RC	Reserve Component
RCM	Requirements Correlation Matrix (AF)
RCS	Radar Cross Section
RDA	Research, Development, and Acquisition
RDT&E	Research, Development, Test, and Evaluation
RFB	Request for Bid
RFI	Ready for Issue; Request for Information
RFP	Request for Proposal
RFQ	Request for Quotation
RIW	Reliability Improvement Warranty
RMA	Revolution in Military Affairs
ROI	Return on Investment
ROM	Read-Only Memory; Rough Order of Magnitude
RRC	Requirements Review Council (Army)
RSI	Rationalization, Standardization, and Interoperability
RTO	Responsible Test Organization

S

S&T	Science and Technology
S/V	Survivability/Vulnerability
SA	Secretary of the Army; Systems Analysis, Supportability Analysis
SAC	Senate Appropriations Committee
SADBU	Small and Disadvantaged Business Utilization
SAE	Service Acquisition Executive
SAF	Secretary of the Air Force
SAF(AQ)	Assistant Secretary of the Air Force (Acquisition)
SAG	Study Advisory Group (Army)
SAIE	Special Acceptance and Inspection Equipment
SAIP	Spares Acquisition Integrated With Production
SAMP	Single Acquisition Management Plan (USAF)
SAP	Special Access Program
SAR	Selected Acquisition Report; Subsequent Application Review; Safety Assessment Report; Special Access Required
SARC	Systems Acquisition Review Council
SASC	Senate Armed Services Committee
SATCOM	Satellite Communications

SBA	Small Business Administration; Simulation Based Acquisition
SBC	Senate Budget Committee
SBIR	Small Business Innovation Research (Program); Space Based Infrared (System) (AF)
SCBCA	Small Claims Board of Contract Appeals
SCCB	Software Configuration Control Board
SCE	Software Capability Evaluation
SCIB	Ships Characteristics and Improvement Board (Navy)
SCMP	Software Configuration Management Plan
SCN	Specification Change Notice; Shipbuilding and Conversion, Navy (Appropriation); Software Change Notice
SD	System Demonstration work effort (part of the System Development and Demonstration phase)
SDB	Small Disadvantaged Business
SDBUP	Small Disadvantaged Business Utilization Program
SDCE	Software Development Capability Evaluation
SDD	System Development and Demonstration (phase of the life cycle)
SDF	Software Development File
SDL	Software Development Library/Laboratory
SDP	Software Development Plan
SDR	Software Design Review
SE	Systems Engineering, Support Equipment
SECDEF	Secretary of Defense
SECNAV	Secretary of the Navy
SECNAVINST	Secretary of the Navy Instruction
SEM (Navy)	Systems Engineering Management; Standard Equipment Modules
SEMP	Systems Engineering Management Plan
SEP	System Engineering Process
SERD	Support Equipment Requirements Document
SETA	Systems Engineering and Technical Assistance
SFR	System Functional Review
SI	Software Item (aka CSCI); System Integration work effort (part of the System Development and Demonstration phase)
SIC	Standard Industrial Classification
SIGINT	Signal Intelligence
SIGSEC	Signal Security
SISMS	Standard Integrated Support Management System
SLEP	Service Life Extension Program
SLOC	Source Lines of Code
SMC	Space and Missile Systems Center (AF)
SMDP	Standardized Military Drawing Program
SMDC	Space and Missile Defense Command (Army)
SMI	Soldier-Machine Interface (Army)
SMIP	Spares Management Improvement Program
SOC	Special Operations Command

SOF	Special Operations Forces
SOO	Statement of Objectives
SOP	Standing Operating Procedure
SOS	System of Systems
SOW	Statement of Work
SPAWAR	Space and Naval Warfare Systems Command
SPC	Statistical Process Control
SPD	System Program Director (AF)
SPE	Senior Procurement Executive
SPEC	Specification
SPI	Single Process Initiative
SPM	System Program Manager (AF); Software Programmer's Manual
SPO	System Program/Project Office (AF)
SPS	Software Product Specification
SQEP	Software Quality Evaluation Plan
SQL	Structured Query Language
SRA	Shop Replaceable Assembly
SRR	System Requirements Review
SRS	Software Requirement Specification
SRU	Subassembly Repairable Unit/Shop Replaceable Unit
SSA	Source Selection Authority; Software Support Agency
SSAC	Source Selection Advisory Council
SSC	Soldier Systems Command (Army)
SSEB	Source Selection Evaluation Board
SSET	Source Selection Evaluation Team
SSG	Special Study Group (Army)
SSP	Source Selection Plan
SSPM	Software Standards and Procedures Manual
SSR	Software Specification Review
SSS	System/Subsystem Specification
SSWG	System Safety Working Group
STA	System Threat Assessment
STAR	System Threat Assessment Report
STA&P	System Threat Assessment and Projections
STANAG	Standardization Agreement (NATO)
STD	Standard; Software Test Description
STE	Special Test Equipment
STEP	Simulation, Test, and Evaluation Process
STLDD	Software Top-Level Design Document
STP	Software Test Plan
STPR	Software Test Procedures
STR	Software Test Report; Software Trouble Report
STRICOM	Simulation, Training and Instrumentation Command (Army)
SUM	Software User's Manual
SUPSHIP	Supervisor of Shipbuilding, Conversion and Repair
SVR	System Verification Review; Shop Visit Rate

SW or S/W	Software
SWARF	Senior Warfighter Forum
SWCI	Software Configuration Item
SW-CMM	Software Capability Maturity Model
SYSCOM	Systems Command (Navy)

T

T&E	Test and Evaluation
TAA	Total Army Analysis
TAACOM	Theater Army Area Command
TACOM	Tank-automotive and Armament Command (Army)
TAAF	Test, Analyze, and Fix
TAD	Technology Area Descriptions
TADSS	Training Aids, Devices, Simulations and Simulators
TAFIM	Technical Architecture Framework for Information Management
TAFT	Test, Analyze, Fix, and Test
TARA	Technology Area Review and Assessment
TAV	Total Asset Visibility
TBD	To be determined/developed
TBIM	Trigger Based Item Management
TC	Type Classification (Army)
TCO	Termination Contracting Officer
TD	Test Director; Technical Data; Technical Director
TDP	Technical Data Package; Test Design Plan
TE	Test Equipment
TECHEVAL	Technical Evaluation (Navy)
TECHMOD	Technology Modernization
TEMP	Test and Evaluation Master Plan
TEMSE	Technical and Managerial Support Environment
TIARA	Tactical Intelligence and Related Activities
TIM	Technical Interchange Meeting
TINA	Truth in Negotiation Act
TIWG	Test Integration Working Group (Army)
TLS	Time Line Sheet
TM	Technical Manual; Technical Management
TMDE	Test, Measurement, and Diagnostic Equipment
TMP	Technical Management Plan
TO	Technical Order
TOA	Total Obligation Authority; Table of Allowance
TOC	Total Ownership Cost
TPM	Technical Performance Measurement
TPS	Test Program Set; Test Package Set
TPWG	Test Planning Working Group (AF)
TRL	Technology Readiness Level
TQM	Total Quality Management

TRACE	Total Risk Assessing Cost Estimating
TRADOC	Training and Doctrine Command (Army)
TRD	Technical Requirements Document
TRR	Test Readiness Review
TSIR	Total System Integration Responsibility
TSM	TRADOC System Manager
TSPR	Total System Performance Responsibility

U

UCR	Unit Cost Report
UDF	Unit Development Folder
UE	Unit Equipment
UI	Unit of Issue
UNK/UNKS	Unknown Unknowns
UNSECNAV	Under Secretary of the Navy
UPS	Uniform Procurement System
USA	United States Army/Under Secretary of the Army
USAF	United States Air Force
USASAC	U.S. Army Security Assistance Center
USC	United States Code
USCG	United States Coast Guard
USD(C)	Under Secretary of Defense (Comptroller)
USD(AT&L)	Under Secretary of Defense (Acquisition, Technology and Logistics)
USD(P&R)	Under Secretary of Defense (Personnel and Readiness)
USD(P)	Under Secretary of Defense (Policy)
USG	U.S. Government
USJFCOM	U.S. Joint Forces Command
USMC	U.S. Marine Corps
USN	U.S. Navy
USSOCOM	United States Special Operations Command
UUT	Unit Under Test

V

V&V	Verification and Validation
VAMOSC	Visibility and Management of O&S Costs
VC	Variable Cost
VCJCS	Vice Chairman, Joint Chiefs of Staff
VCNO	Vice Chief of Naval Operations (Navy)
VCSA	Vice Chief of Staff (Army)
VCSAF	Vice Chief of Staff (AF)
VDD	Version Description Document
VE	Value Engineering
VECP	Value Engineering Change Proposal
VHSIC	Very High Speed Integrated Circuit

VLSI	Very Large Scale Integration

W

WAN	Wide Area Network
WARM	Wartime Reserve Modes
WBS	Work Breakdown Structure
WCF	Working Capital Funds
WIPT	Working-Level Integrated Product Team
WMD	Weapons of Mass Destruction
WP/N	Weapons Procurement (Appropriation), Navy
WPI	Wholesale Price Index
WSIG	Weapon Support Improvement Group (OSD)
WSMP	Weapon System Master Plan (AF)
WTCV	Weapons and Tracked Combat Vehicles (Appropriation)(Army)

Y

Y2K	Year 2000

Other

3GL	Third Generation Language
4GL	Fourth Generation Language
5GL	Fifth Generation Language
5Ms	Machinery, Manpower, Material, Measurement and Method
8A	Section 8A of the Small Business Act pertaining to minority and other disadvantaged businesses

Made in the USA
Lexington, KY
07 May 2011